THE TANGLE OF MEANINGS
A BOOK OF POETRY AND PAINTINGS
Black & White Edition

by *Patrick J. Leach*

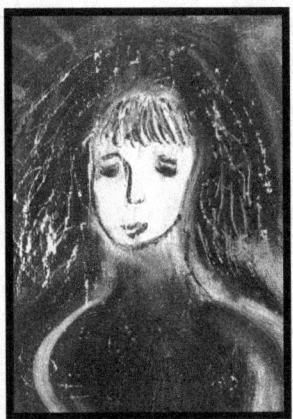

Copyright © 2013 by Patrick J. Leach

ISBN: 9781477596548

CreateSpace, North Charleston, SC

The Tangle of Meanings
dedicated to Joanne Sullivan
                    Donald Baxter
                    Rick Perkins
Friends and confidants no longer with us
except in memory and love.

I appreciate their love, wisdom,
Sobriety, and belief in my
Spiritual and artistic journey,
Always encouraging and hopeful.
God Bless...

Poetry and paintings by Patrick J. Leach

Photography by David DeWert

Design by Angela Longovia and
         Patrick J. Leach

Editing by Linda Anglin

Acknowledgements to Linda Anglin, my spiritual and personal supporter in art and writing this last 4 years, A.R. Ammons and William Matthews for poetry writing classes many years ago at Cornell University, and so many others in my life who have supported me in my art and writing efforts, and to God, that wonderful and mysterious entity so much at work in my life and art, my anchor to what it is to be a human being in this vast, vast ocean of life. Many thanks to Angela Longovia for her excellent work doing the computer layout and preparation for printing for this book.

Important Note
Please contact me through my website patleachartist.com to inquire about purchasing paintings, or books, and to offer venues to show my art at galleries, museums and private showings. I welcome your participation in helping me share my art with the world.

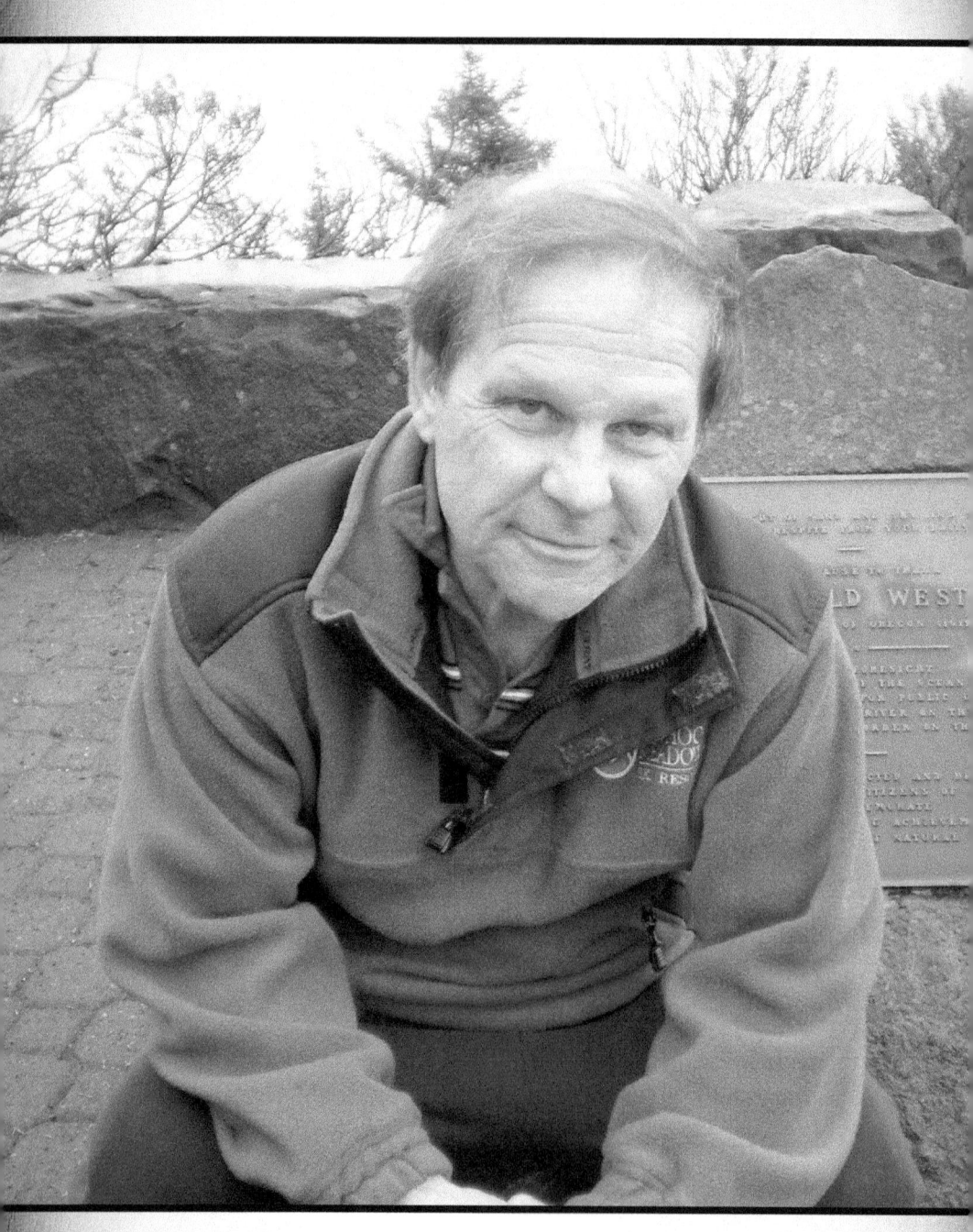

INTRODUCTION

My name is Patrick Leach. This is my second published book of poetry. I have been writing poetry off and on my entire adult life. I studied creative writing at Cornell University, and have written technical manuals, radio and television scripts, business training materials, annual reports, fund raising pieces, am coauthor of a soon to be published biography about artist C.S. Price, and received professional awards for various technical publications. Art came to me later in life and I am very much enthralled with being a painter. The poem in this book titled "The Tangle of Meanings" offers some details about my personal struggles with writing and living.

I believe my inspiration comes from God and take little credit for work represented here beyond pursuing a Bachelor of Science degree from Cornell University and two Master of Arts degrees from Washington State University. I own my own small business caring for people's yards and homes in Portland, Oregon, which affords me freedom to write and paint in my off hours. I am very grateful to the men and women I work for, many of whom have become my friends and offer me glimpses into their lives.

Perhaps the most significant event in my life occurred on July 23, 1995, the date of recovery from addiction to alcohol and recreational drugs. It was followed by cessation of tobacco addiction on May 5, 1997, both events made possible by the grace of God, wise counselors in treatment programs, and other sober people I've grown to love and value.

I believe it is important to communicate from my soul to yours. I enjoy the utility of words to pinpoint meanings more accurately, but love the fluid and untangled freedom from the bondage of reality that painting the kind of abstract art I like to do affords. Unfortunately, the very abstract art I began with and still love to paint is barely represented in this book. It is shown in full color books available for purchase.

I pray for continuing persistence and faith, a very tall order sometimes in the life of this artist. The late professor Ammons, author of over a dozen books of poetry, said to me in his office many years ago "I could have papered my walls with rejection letters before I was able to find my way into print." I am very grateful for everyone who appreciates anything I produce. I sincerely hope it helps someone feel more comfortable and accepted in his or her own skin. This world is so often such a confusing and uninviting place to live without the support and solace we offer one another, in the same way that so many poets and artists have been a lifeline for me.

Contents

Contents *(continued)*

Contents *(continued)*

Contents *(continued)*

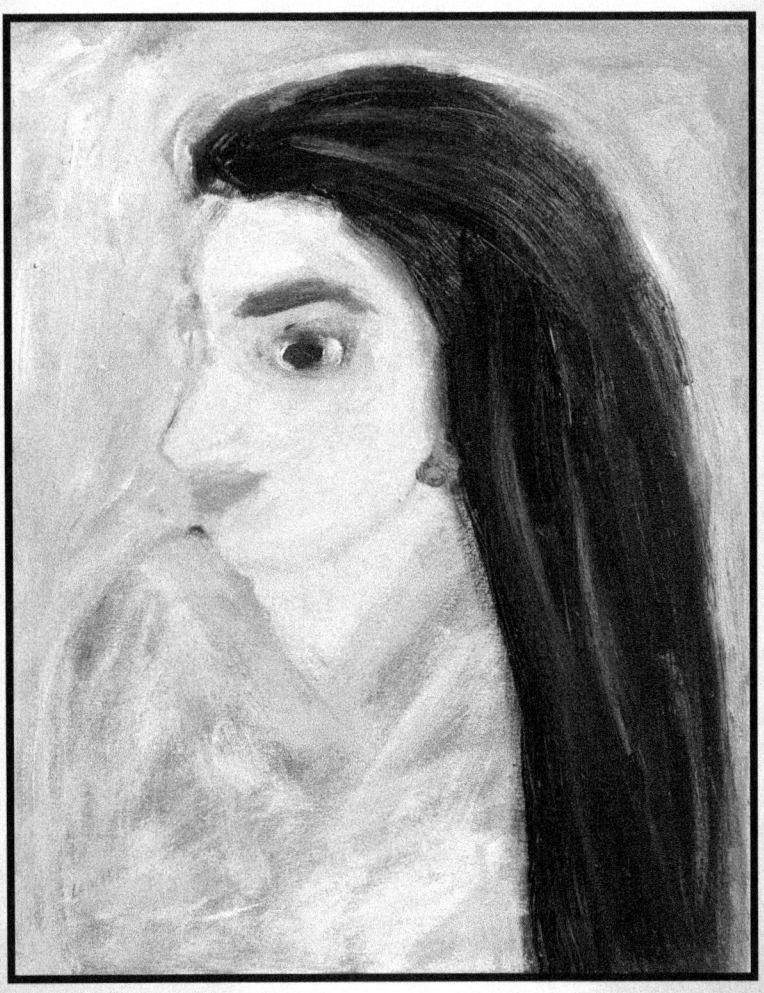

THE TANGLE OF MEANINGS

I gave up writing poetry for decades, it happened slowly
not writing, lost deeper and deeper in alcoholism and addiction;

now 16 years sober, dabbling in it bumping along through this
time writing some poems I like along the way, keeping a daily
journal

Now suddenly feeling the poetry surging in me stronger than
ever since I was a teenager starting college, 61 years old now,
so grateful

I studied with good writing teachers who wrote and published
poetry books at Cornell, Ammons and Matthews, felt confused
after graduation

confused that poetry was not so great a gift or perhaps too
ordinary, unappreciated or I wasn't good enough, so slowly I
left her for some pitiful

reasons and paid the price as a piece of my soul isolated and
imprisoned still alive but sickly, undernourished

now I join with her again welcome her into my life to rejoice
with and embrace her and be the poet I once felt I was destined
to be

not concerned with what she will yield, acknowledging so
often this poetry, like now, is prose and makes too much literal
sense but so be it

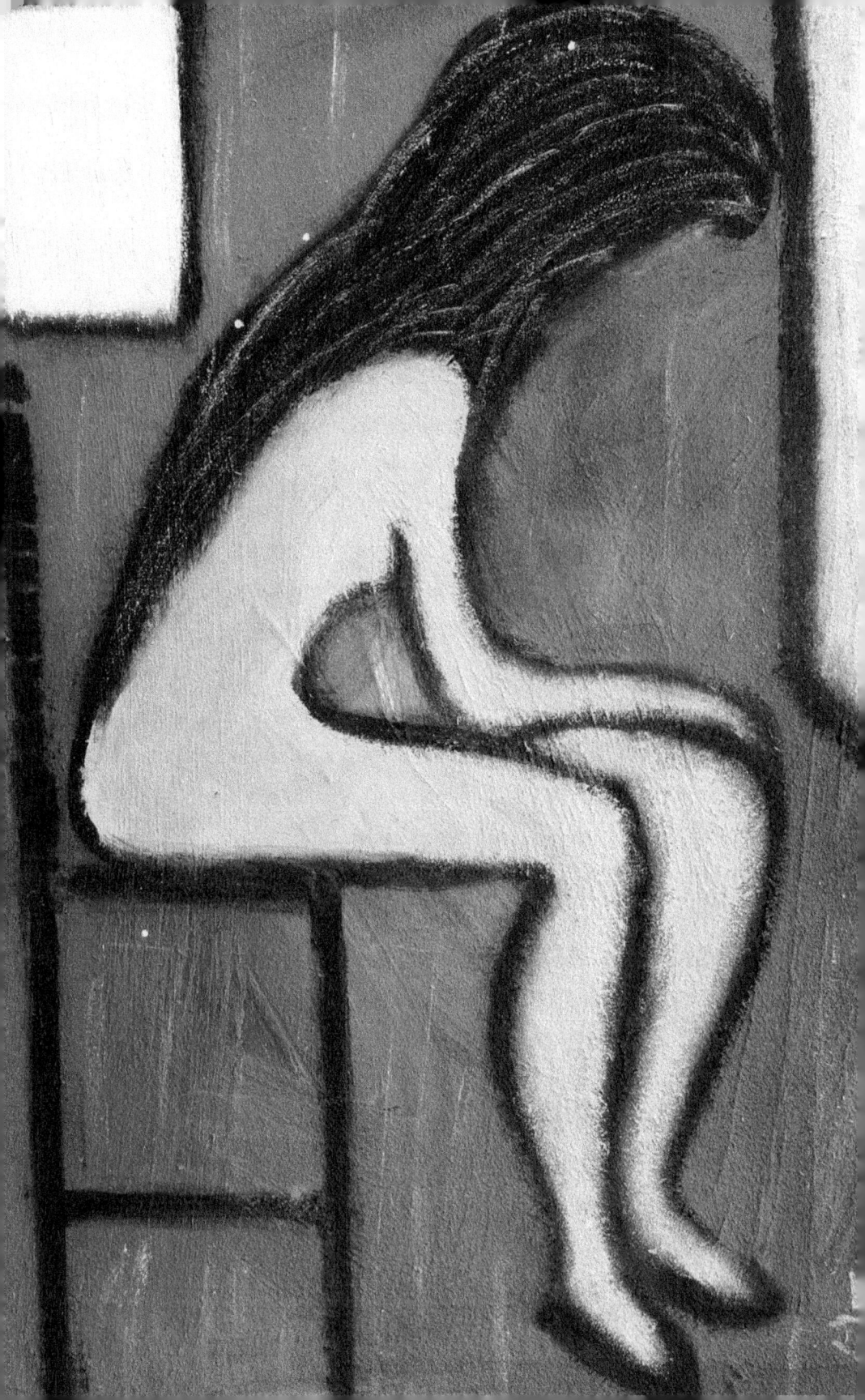

THE TANGLE OF MEANINGS *(continued)*

I like to write this way, not hiding excessively behind twists and turns and purposeful camouflages of meaning, rather revealing what is really going on inside, and for me this helps to say it and to read someone's honest expressions through words and ideas, it helps me survive with dignity of being knowing I am not alone, I am not inferior or worthless, I am worth loving and supporting, as are you…

And yes, it is also so wonderfully freeing to let go the words and paint, yes, letting go of the tangle of meanings for the flow of paint, textures, forms and colors, abstractions; knowing I've often written on the backs of the canvases even as the other side glistened with paint still wet because that urge to write never left me, even in my darkest drunkest ugliest terror filled nights I would try to make some sense in written words of this mystery of being a human being in this time, so grateful I lived through all that and am still healthy and creative, God bless us each and every one I thank this God for making me a sober poet and an artist with a soul that wants to understand who and what I am in this vast and incomprehensible constantly changing insanely beautiful universe that we only visit, briefly, and ever so intimately . . .

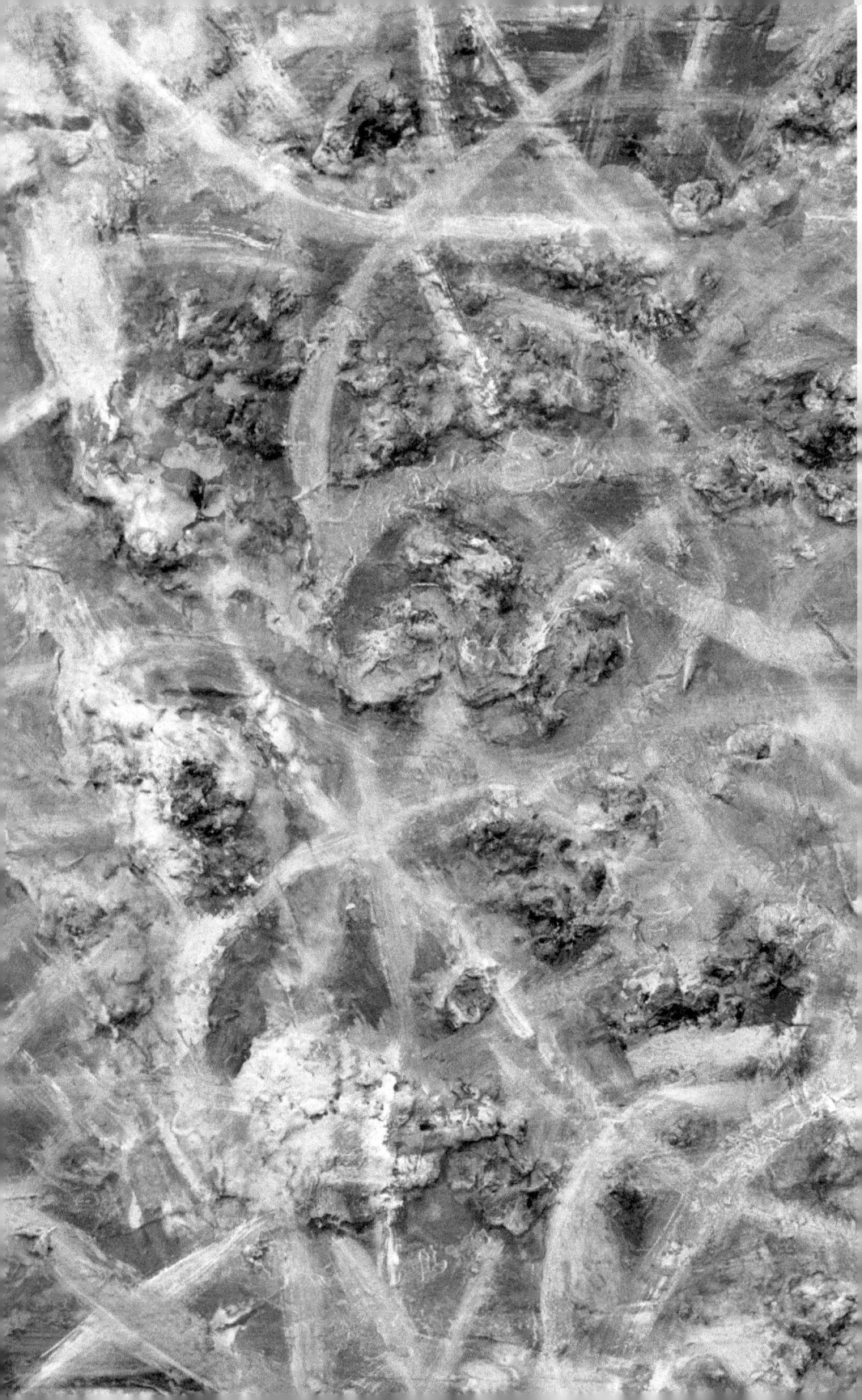

In this little bubble

nice to sit here by the window at my desk

with sunshine and nothing to do but be here

writing when I want to, not worrying about

what is on my list of things to do

just being here with God

this is where I want to be, when I'm at my best

taking time to sit and meditate with my eyes open

setting aside so many petty concerns and irritations

just enjoying this gift of life in this moment

as it moves along on this vast sea of time

living in this little bubble I call me

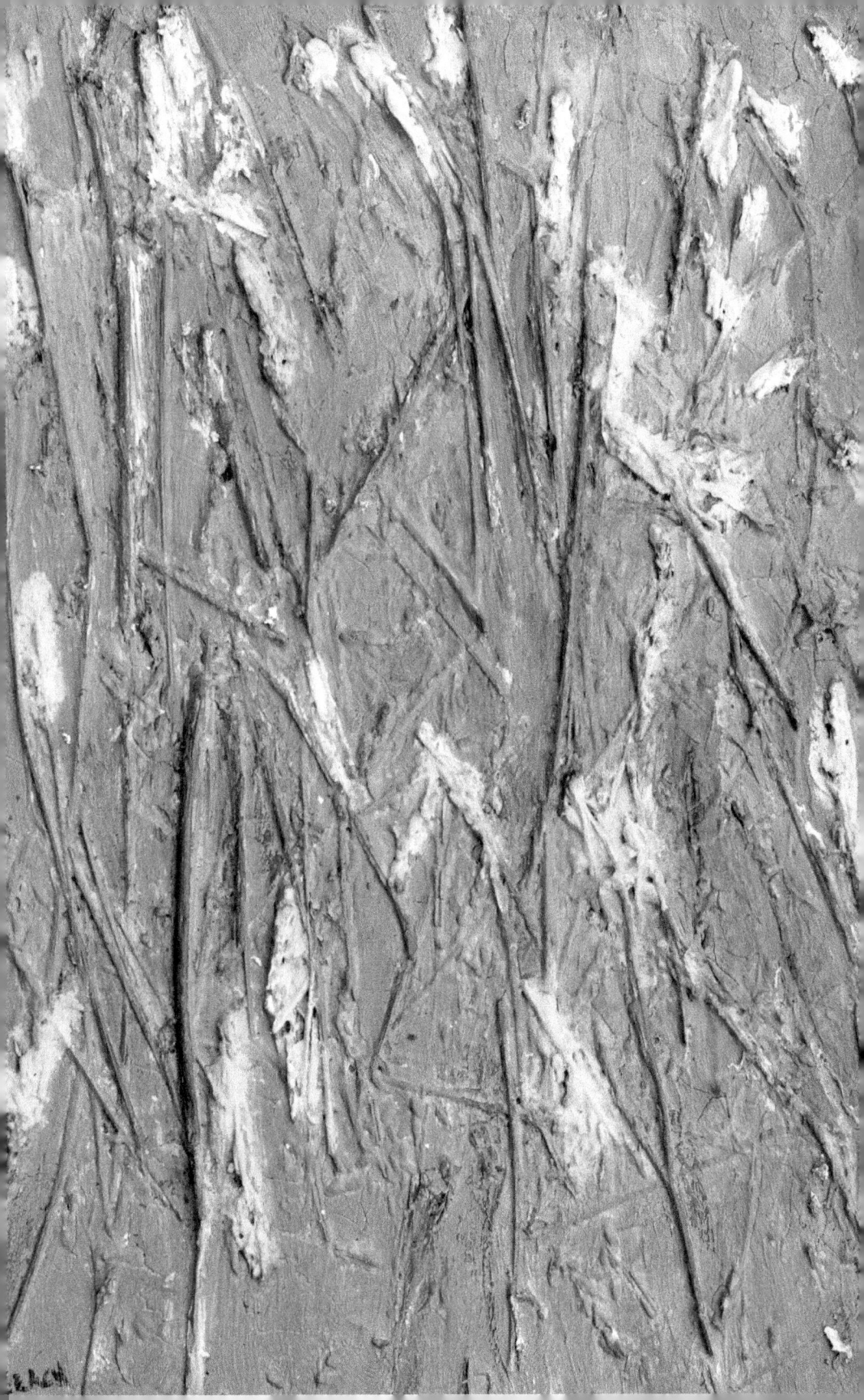

WHAT IS IMPORTANT AND MEANINGFUL?

Expressing the love I feel, being close to that mysterious God
I rely on for so much, being true to Great Spirit in all
relationships

Nurturing spiritual presence by being a good human being
being compassionate and loving and generous, tolerant of
others

Treating other life as I wish to be treated with respect and
kindness
Living up to the commitments I make, and changing those
commitments

When they no longer hold meaning and value
Or when they interfere with what's important

Like a troublesome relationship or a job that wastes my
Talents and aspirations or threatens my integrity

Making myself available to others, their purposes
And dreams, making amends when I fail them or abuse their
good

Praying, meditating, examining, communicating, crying,
laughing,
Respecting, seeking what is important in life

Knowing I have so often failed and will fail again
Being willing to keep on trying until I die

Calling on God to do for me what I cannot do for myself
And getting up each morning grateful for another day

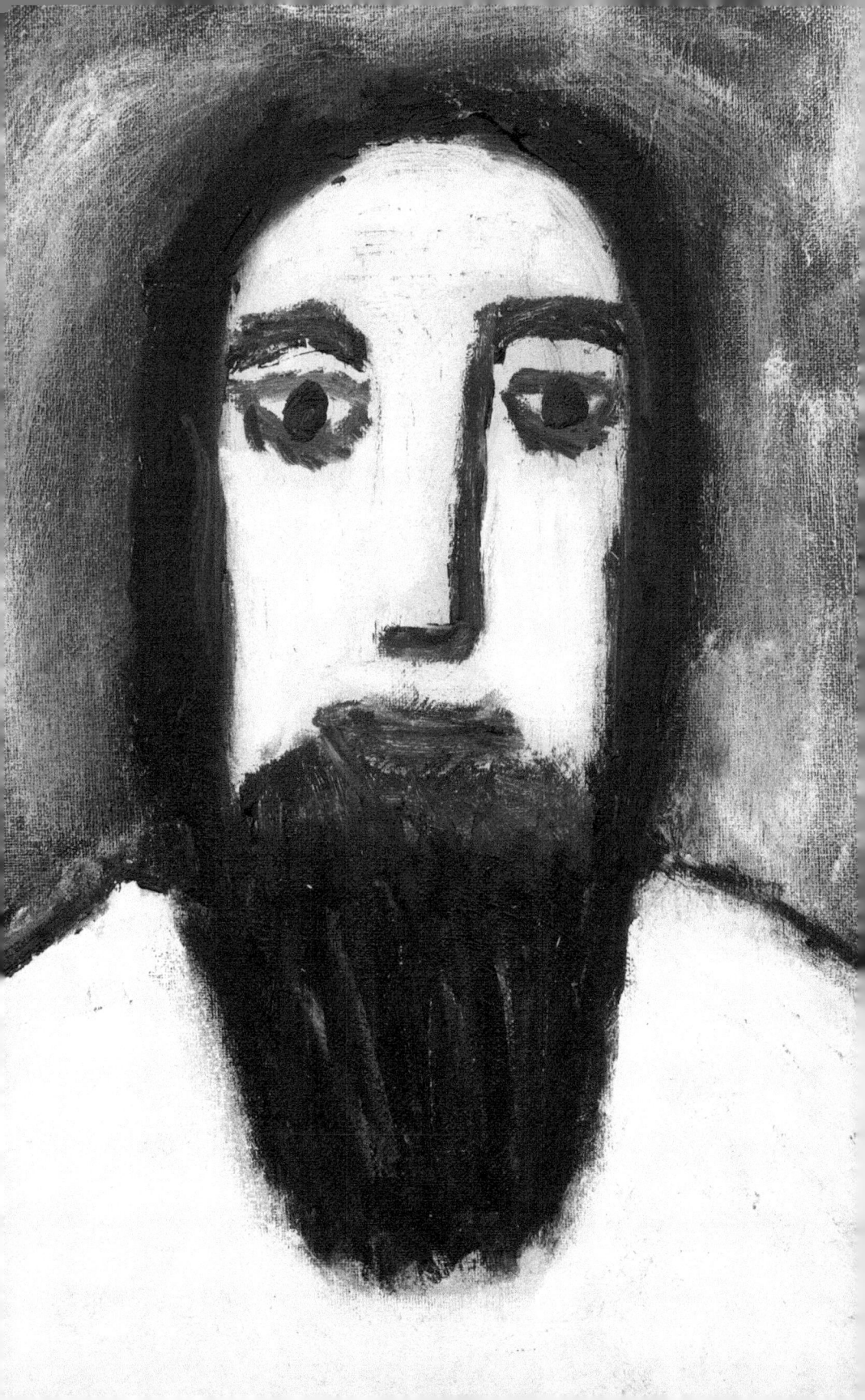

The Trouble With Being A Sober Alcoholic

The trouble with being a sober
alcoholic
Is one slip back into drinking or
drugging begins the whole downward
nightmare all over

Dying instead of living

To drink and take drugs is death to this
Alcoholic

Sobriety please

PLEASE

deliver me, oh God,

from misery

and loneliness

and self

to You

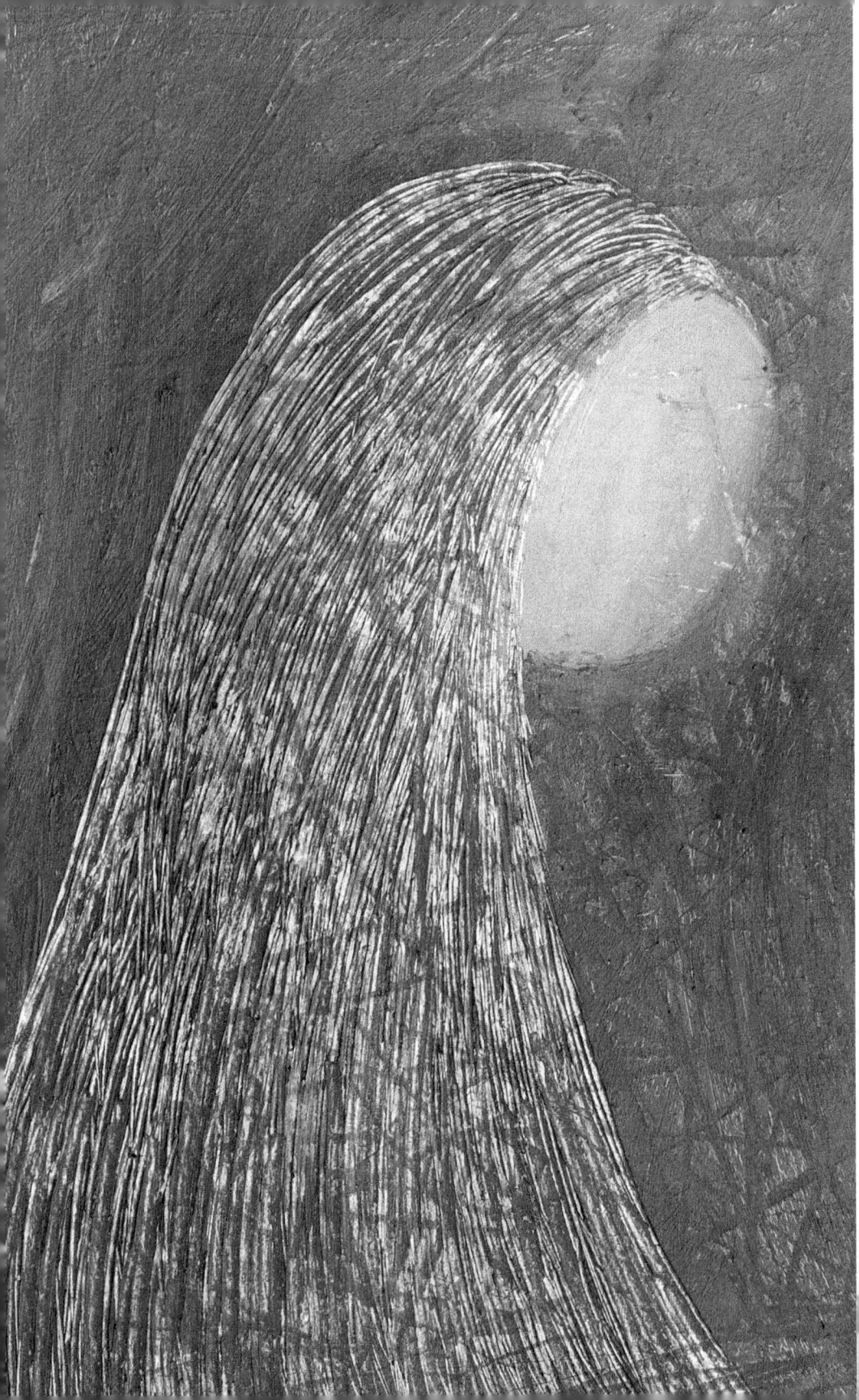

FLEETING IS OUR TIME HERE

We, so vulnerable in bodies of flesh and blood
with minds capable of so much brilliance
and absurdity
of spirits bathed in love and compassion
and hate and war
our strife, our peace
our forgotten abandoned dreams
these brief and incredibly long lives
lived with and against each other
I pray please help me truly live
and experience what I'm here to do
so fleeting is our time here
peering out at our stars and planets
we often miss what is here to enjoy
and focus on what is not to our liking
praying I learn while there is still time
here, in this moment
on this path, in this life
this precious life rejoice with our Creator
being kind to one another . . .

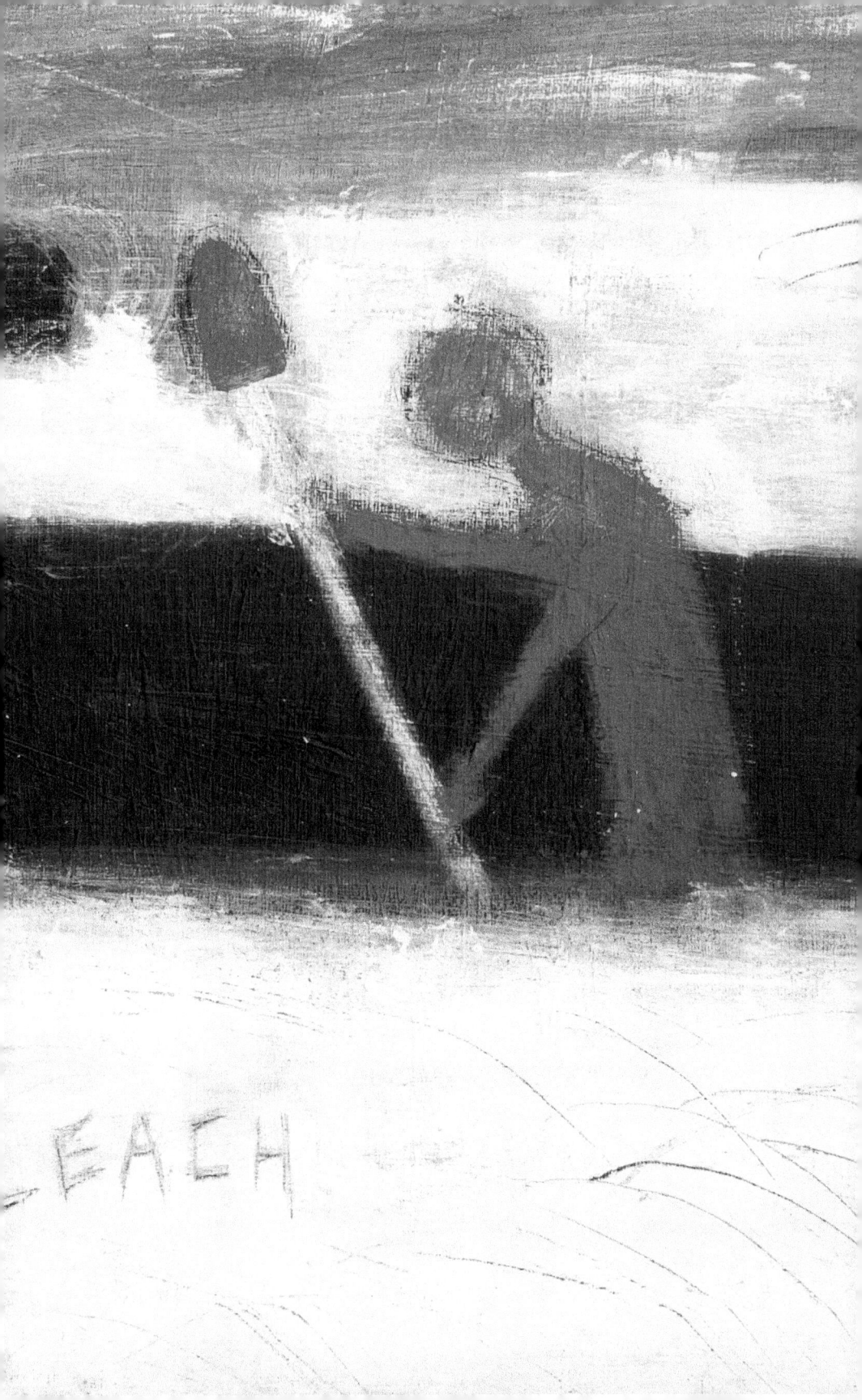

The Song

Hearing beautiful melodic sounds this morning
Sounds I've heard mornings for years

Perhaps decades out back at this time of year
When the sun sits low in a cloud-covered sky

Appreciated songs
Imagining the source a beautiful multicolored

Expansive lovely creature
In my usual hurry to get somewhere quickly

But looking up, searching this morning
Into the bare branches of the trees

There sat a tiny plain drab colored bird
Quivering slightly every time it sang its notes

Waiting to hear similar sounds
From another of its kind, we all wait

Like the little bird, I put out my words to
The world, and I wait

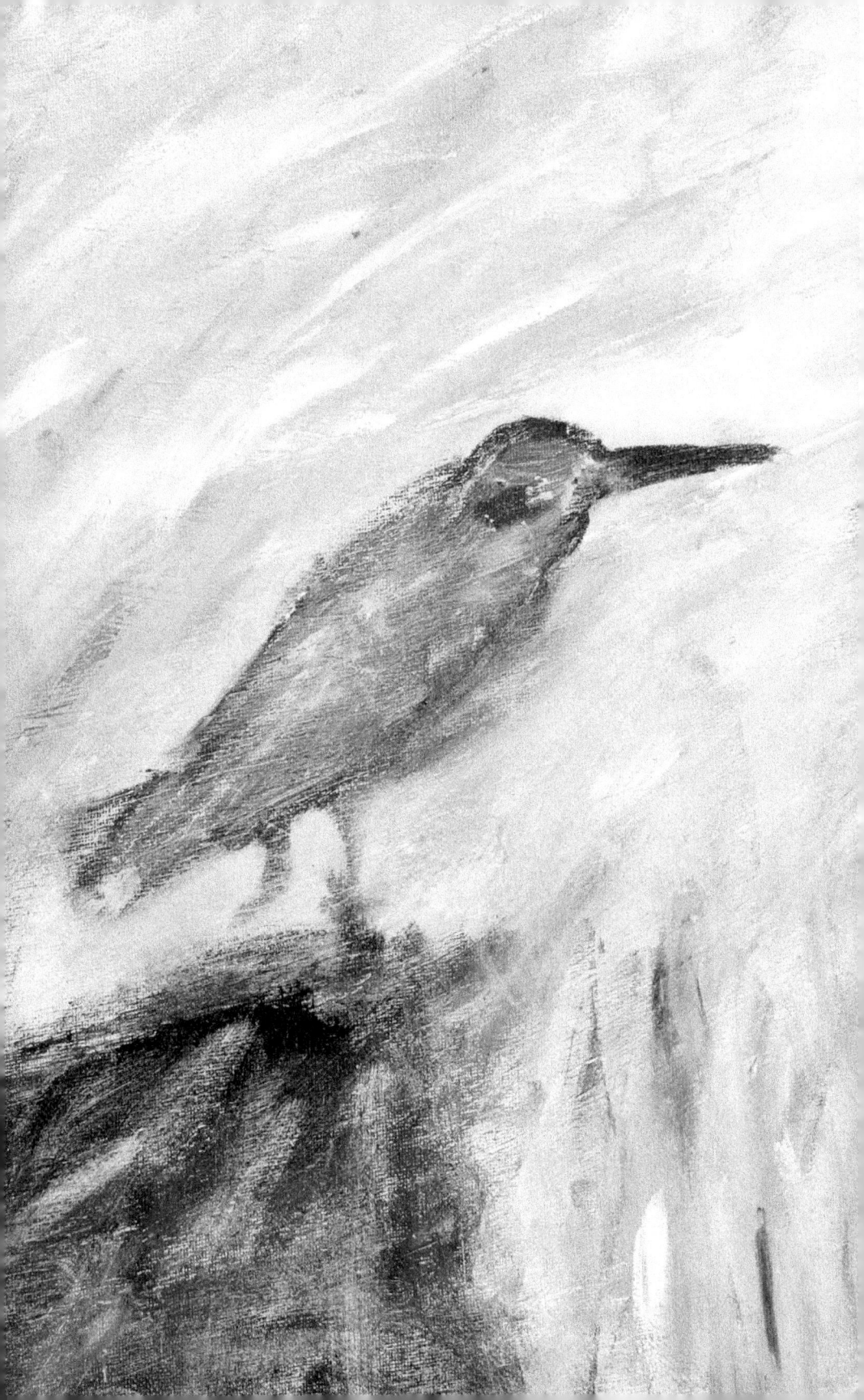

Silent Joy

The long dark cold nights of winter are growing shorter and warmer, I feel the warmth and light of spring life already. Bulbs are pushing up and showing their green leaves, a hint of yellow from the first crocus, birds are singing more often of the renewal that is just ahead. I sing my songs of gratitude and sobriety, hope and joy like gentle rain fallng. I feel Your presence in my life God, offer thanks for these still quiet moments of silent joy feeling the pale sunshine and a gentle breeze.

To God

I will never be able
by my own power alone
to make up for all those
Wasted years drunk
so I give up trying
The goal is to do what I can
Now as one moment passes
into the next, grateful I'm alive,
and enjoy the journey
Home to You

THE MEETING LAST NIGHT

She spoke of the depression, an ongoing
Weight, an anchor to the child's nightmares
No longer valid but refusing to let up

And the lifting, a gale filling the sails
To warmth and gratitude
Freeing both, for an indeterminable time

Resonating with my story my prayers
For freedom from dead weights pulling
Me down God lifting my soul,
Dropping the bottles and desire for the end

How I project to seeing the whole
More clearly, our role in the downing
Of lives around us,
Mysterious how we escape with our sanity

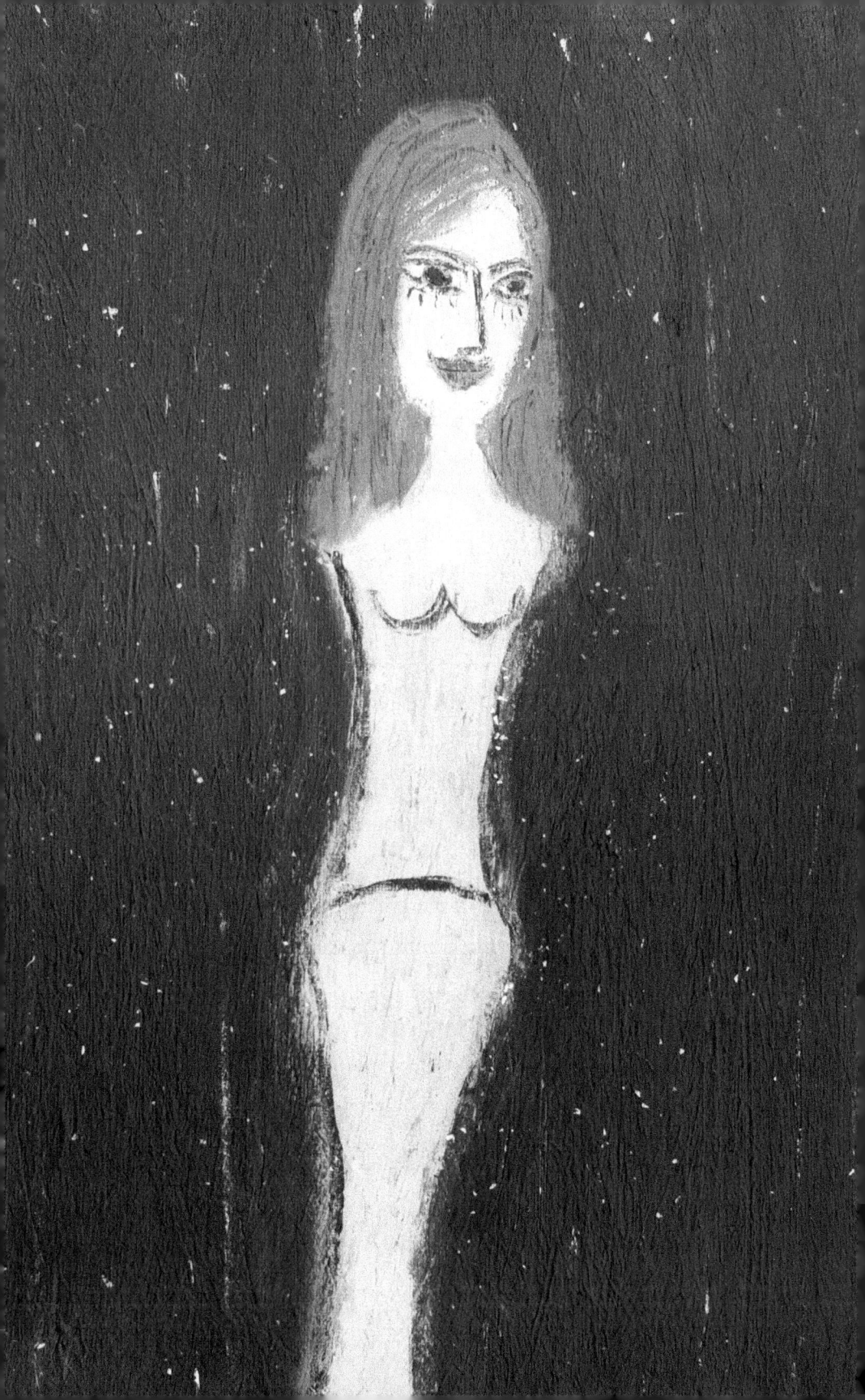

HOME

I settled roots here in this home
decades now and building

living and loving and creating here
praying, meditating, working

This is where I feel safe and secure, I can lock
the doors and keep out the world whenever I want

my sanctuary, my peace to reside here
in this home with solid walls and foundations

roof and basement, garage, large green grass yard
my garden and trees, to live here is such a joy

to care for this home, such a sweet and pleasant place
to live, even the sound of saying, home, brings peace of mind
and soul…

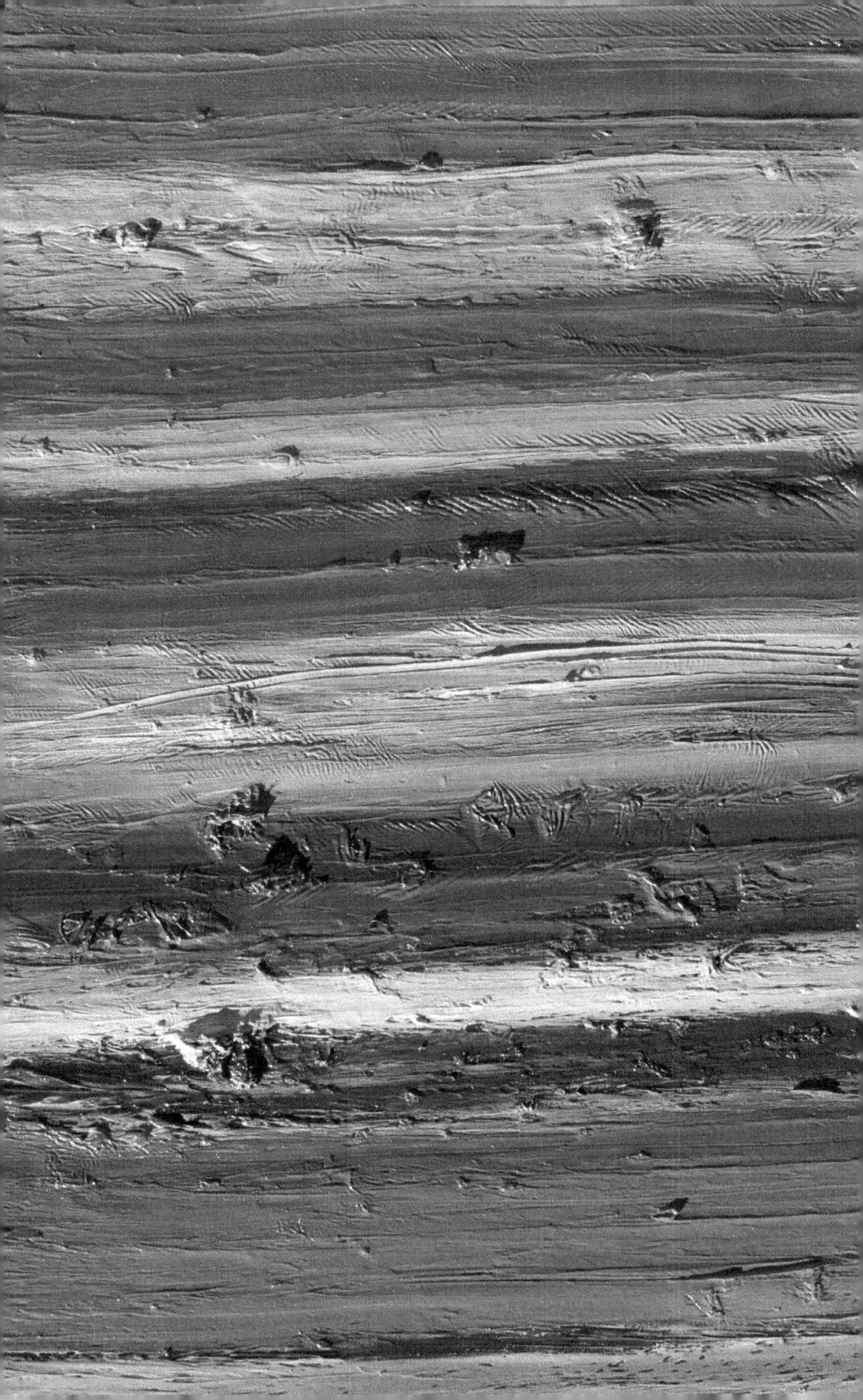

There Once Lived A Man

there once lived a man
who thought he was better than
other men

He lived his life in poverty
Separated, aloof from everyone
Else; they all knew he thought

He was better than them
And they stayed away
Whenever anyone tried to love him

He always held back
Afraid to lose himself in someone
Else, the spiritual imperfection of

Union with another human being
So he lived his life in poverty
Dying inside of loneliness and separation

From God
And you
And the rest of us

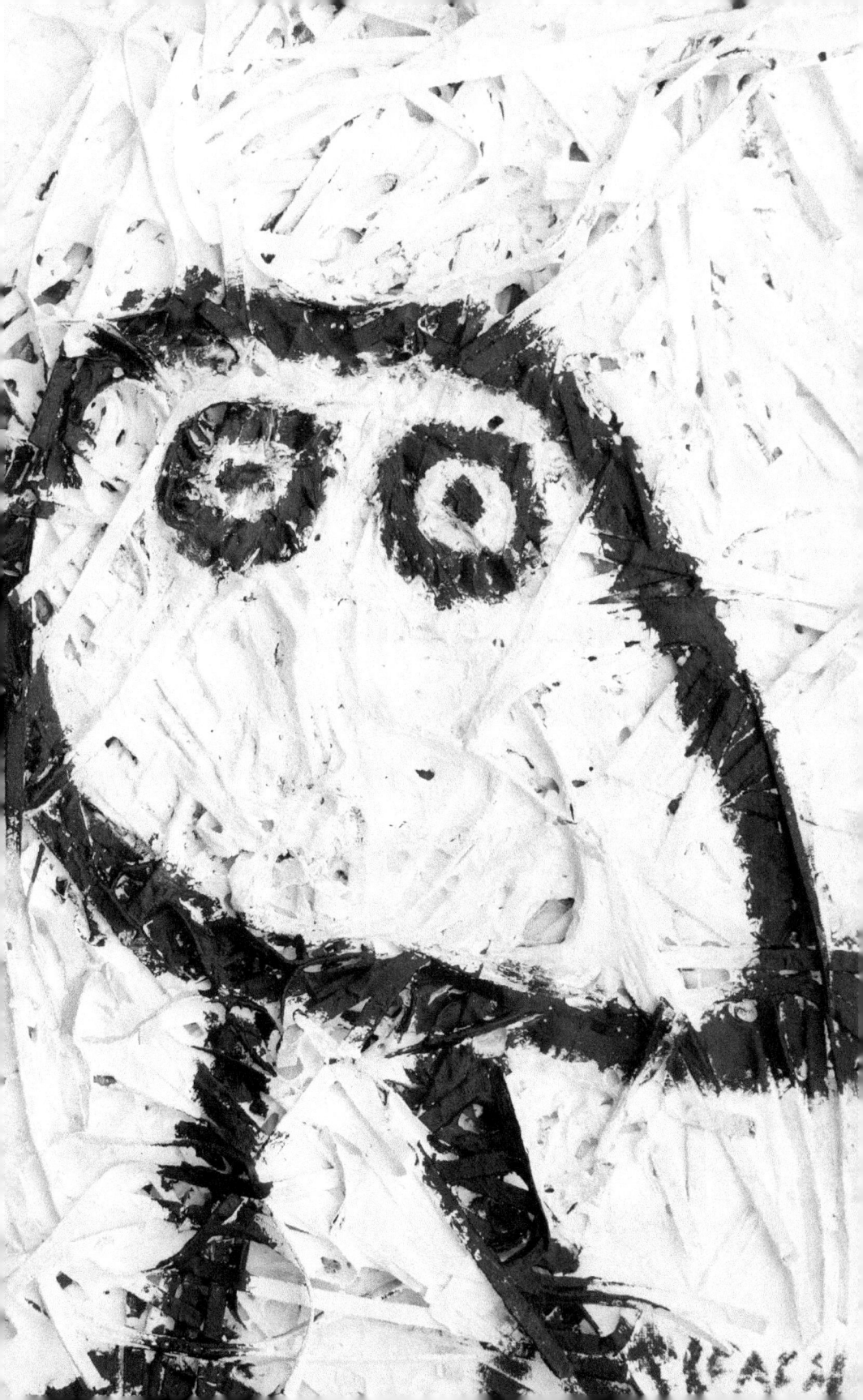

A Gift of the Divine

Such a rough way to start life
Living under the heavy handed abuse
And insanity of the family-isms
Taking on the weight inside the isms
Growing up into a twisted crooked man

And then came intervention of the Spirit
We call divine
Unexpected, sublime
Working on a masterpiece
Its unique and tangled ways

Celebrating life
A gift of the divine

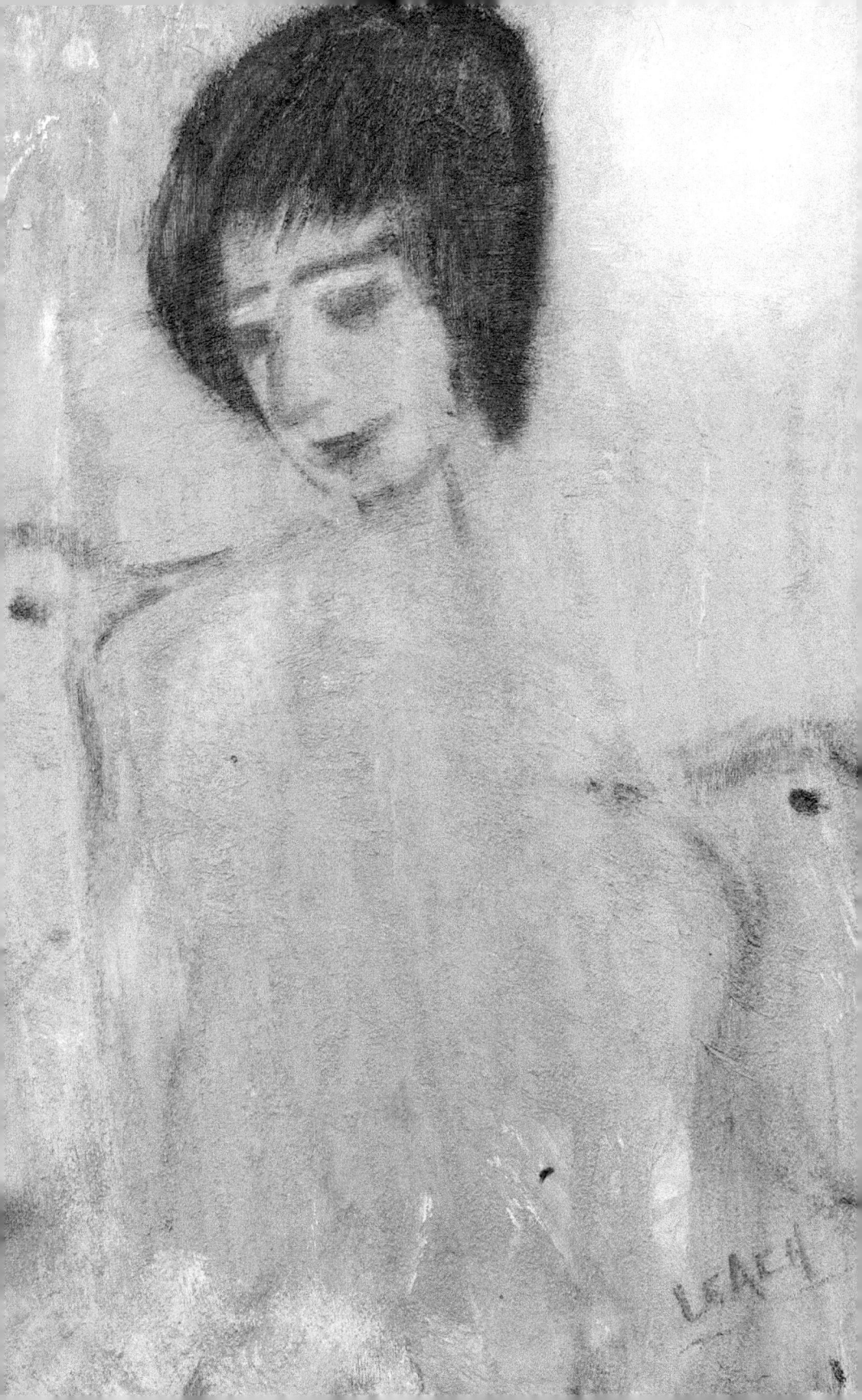

Better days

There were days I dreaded
Getting out of bed, facing
A new day, alone, depressed

Troubled by a bad job, a bad
relationship, no relationship,
Bad feelings about myself
and what I was doing
to myself

I'm grateful those days are
passed, not that I always
Spring out of bed
happy, but the dread and
terrible months long
depression slowly left me
when I stopped drinking
and smoking pot

And for this and so much
more, I am grateful

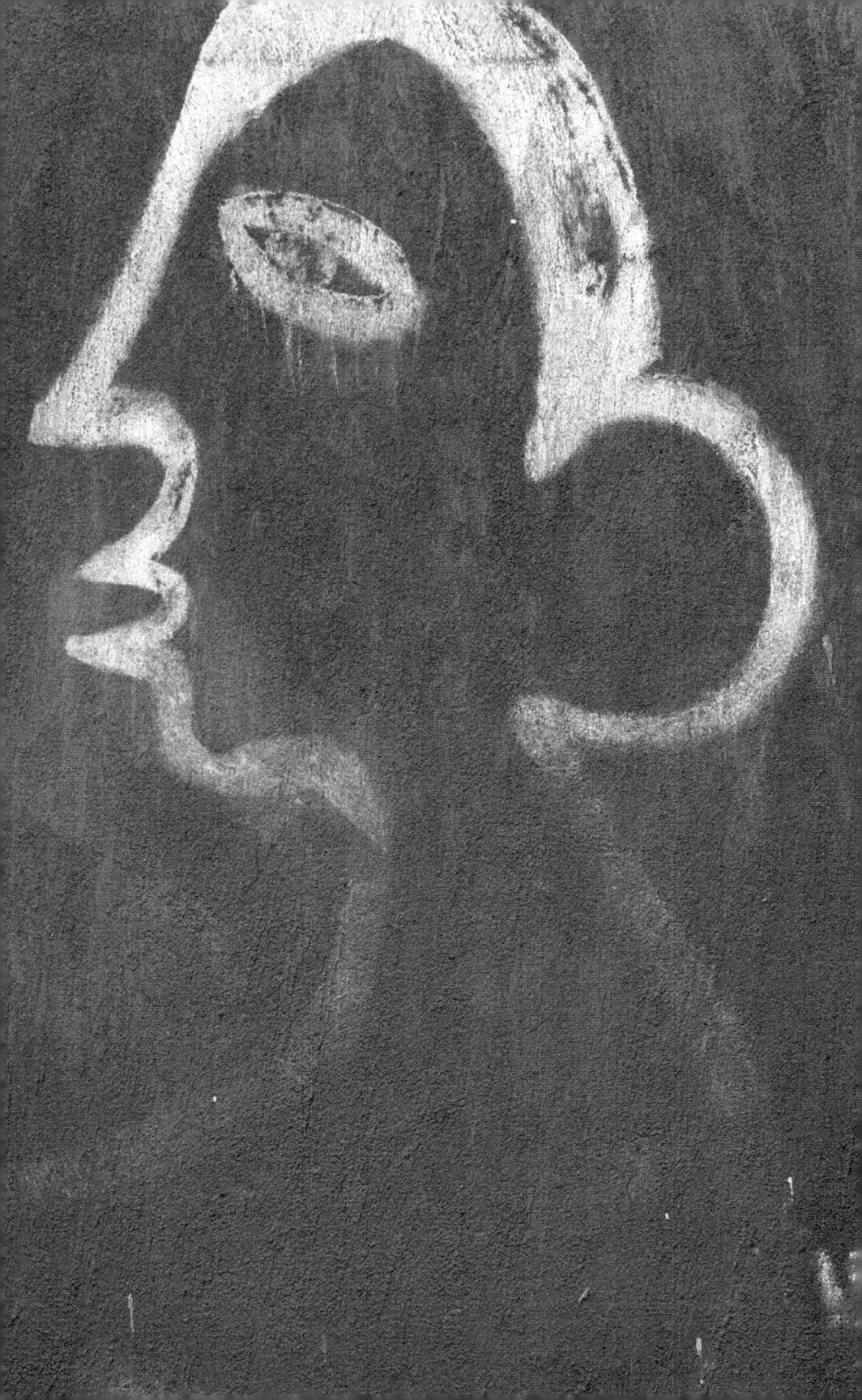

Knowing I'm Not The Only One

We were playing with her little dog outside who took my

Treats at a distance, nervous and fearful of me

"It takes a long time for her to warm up and trust anyone"

I laughed "I'm like that too"

She whispered "Me too"

And we looked at each other and smiled at this big truth shared,

Over such a little thing

Feeling a little less out of place in the world

Sometimes so strange in my own skin trying to understand

Why I am the way I am, often not meeting my own

expectations

About how I should be

It helps knowing I'm not the only one

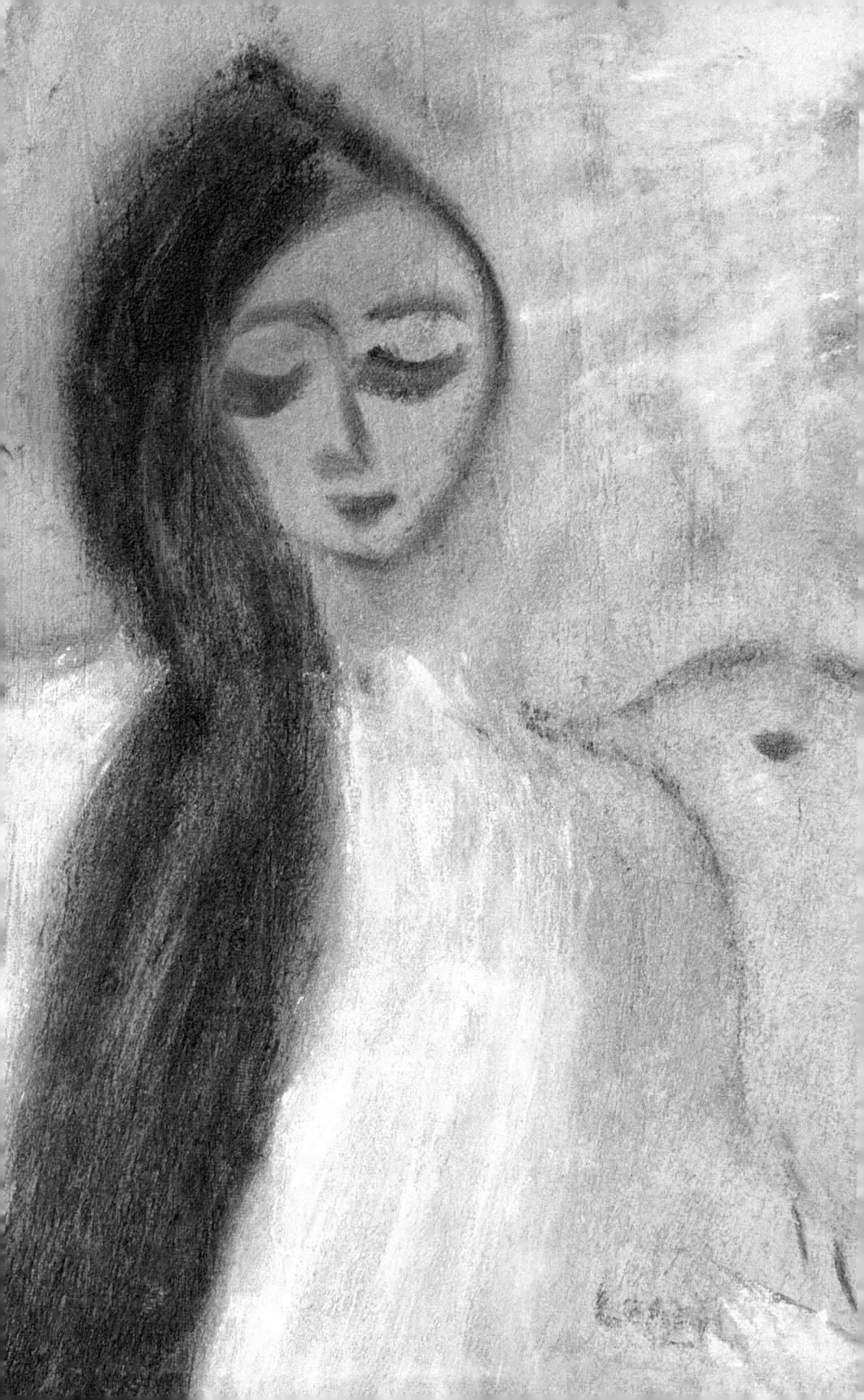

The world is a wheel

The world is a moving rotating
round circular spherical cylindrical wheel
always moving round and round
going nowhere
really fast
but never still

We live our lives on the wheel
birth to death wondering
were we ever real

The world is on my side I think
going round and round always
moving round

Hunger

there is a hunger in me
a mystery I long for
turning my face, searching
hunting for something
the shape of it, texture, substance
I cannot grasp
with hands or mind

a hunger for things
unseen
in body and soul
inviting it into me
closer
more complete

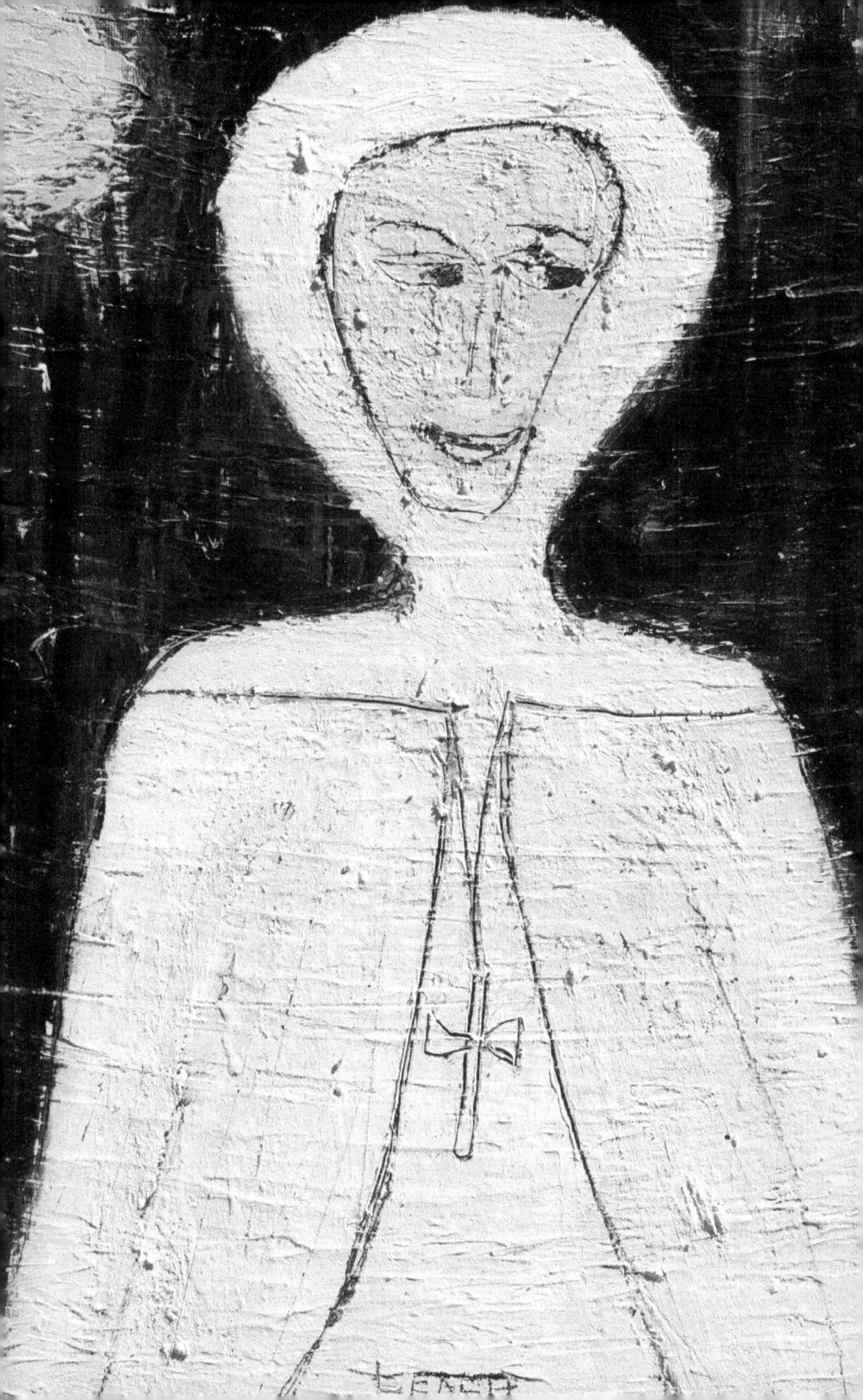

The Trouble with Intimate Relationships

Those unsolvable problems that are so clear after a few years of intimacy, the things we cannot or will not give to our partner

Our refusal or inability to change to meet their needs, Theirs to ours

Worrying about their welfare and wanting to give advice and facilitate change

Yes, no, yes, no, no, no

Until after awhile it is easier and less painful to walk away and be alone without the intimacy as is my pattern over and over in my life

The trouble with intimate relationships for me is that I prefer my own company when problems won't go away in relationship with another person

And I get so lonely sometimes . . .

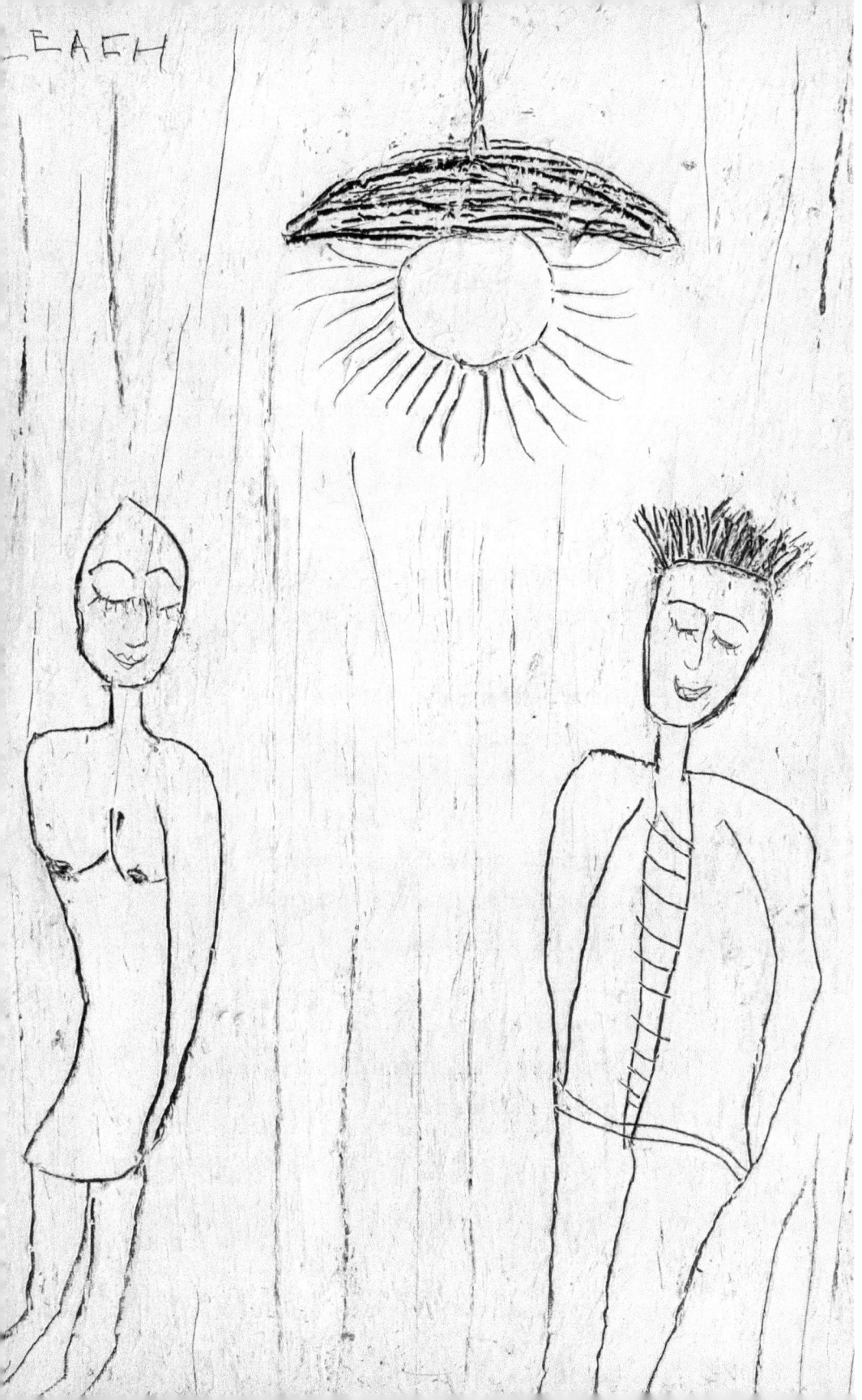

Great Dams Inside

Someone built great dams in my mind,
Thoughts built up and flooded back into
All the tributaries and open spaces inside

In the alcoholic ward the doctors and
Nurses treated my disease
Opened blockages, worked on my

Years in the making, settled in
Raised the dams slowly, loosened up
Rivers of thought and poetry

Art and words breaking like winter
Ice on a frozen river, the spring thaw
Is on and this is what I see

Flowing out of me, knowing now
Drugs cloud and silt and flood the mind
And God set me free

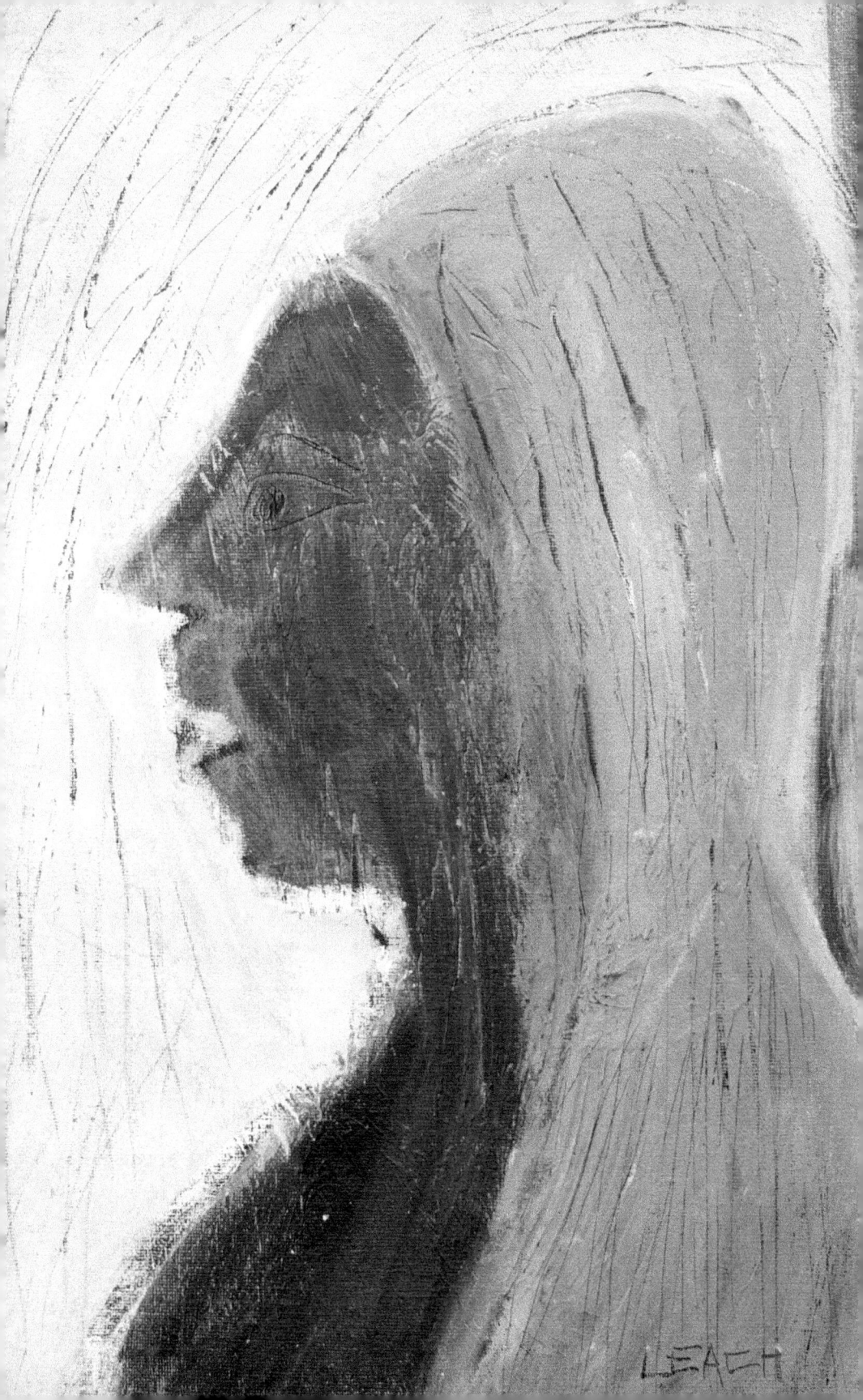

DO NOT MOURN MY PASSING

Please, do not mourn my passing
This beautiful wonderful rare gift of life
With its all consuming wonder and involvement
Enchantment and pains
Moves lightly from me to you and our passing
generation
Our ancestors yield to us
And we to you of our future
We live and die in such short time frames
Yet it feels at times we are so ancient
Fall victim to life's lies and fallacies
Not hearing the beat of God's heart
and soul within us
We all come here to live in these bodies of flesh and
Blood, return to ashes after death
Such integral parts of the whole
And search for our connections with
God so close to us into us permeating
Every cell within
So far away we cannot see or touch
Thank You God our unexpected and rare
Gifts of life
Of deep meaning and perpetuity
With my passing I return somehow home
As God would have me
And then to You your gift of life

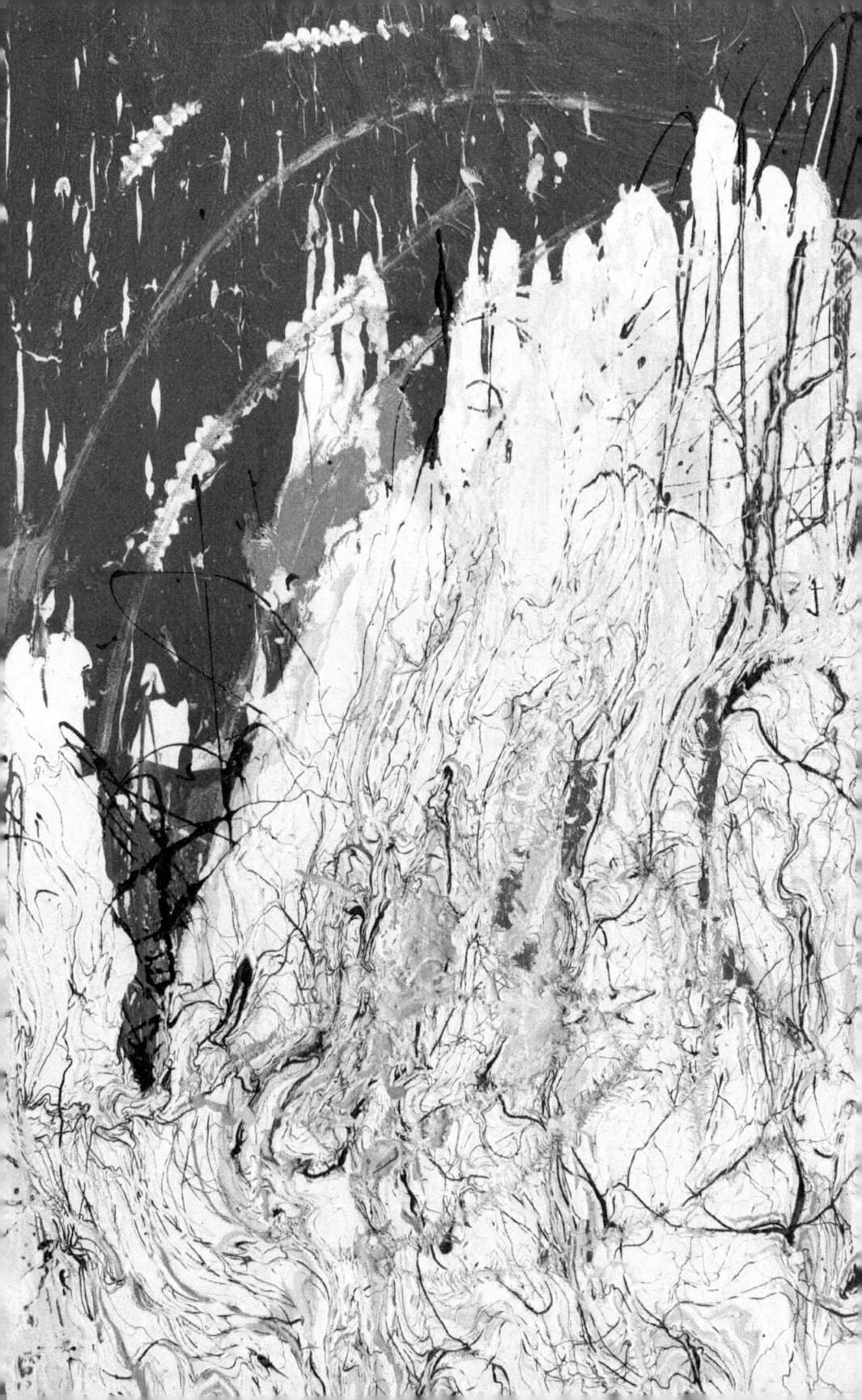

THIS LIFE IS MYSTERY

This life is mystery
So painful and confusing at times
So lonely and frustrating
Without hope or guarantee of permanent improvement
All mixed up together in the aloneness and chaos I call me
Staring into eternity so black and immense
With only stars and each other to guide our way
My being so small and alone divided and separate
Comforted by faith in oneness with God's spirit
That all is well despite the vexations of reason
And selfish obsession
Oh God I pray sincerely for each and everyone
Such small physical boats on such overwhelming
And threatening seas
With our life's end so inevitable and mysterious
And yet with all these feelings and insecurities I
Offer heartfelt thanks this awesome gift of life…

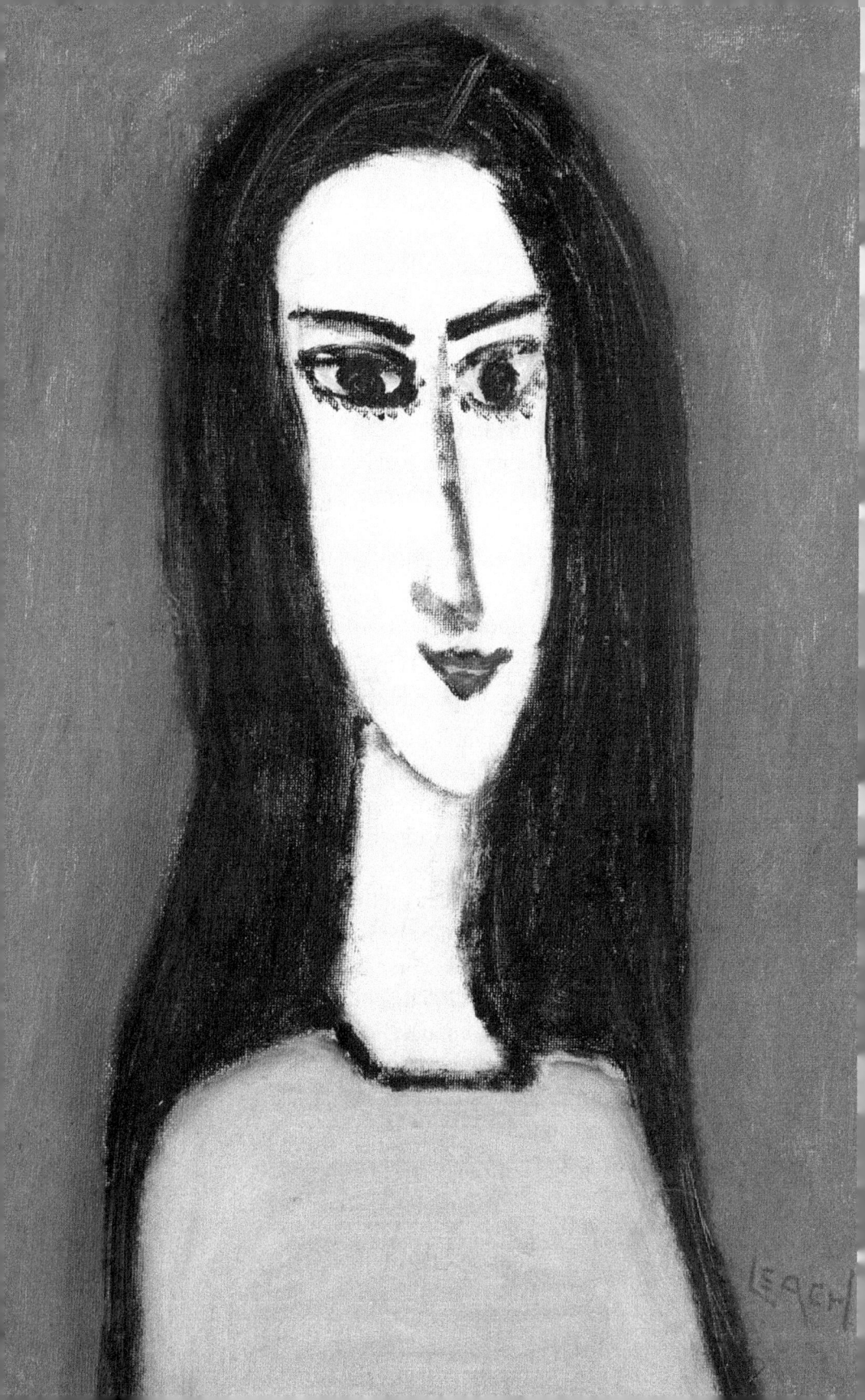

THESE THINGS I WILL MISS

The sounds of crickets on a warm summer night
Fireflies dancing and moving through the velvet darkness
The way the ocean sounds as it moves
Wind in the trees, the way clouds pass over the sun
The way the moon looks all yellow and huge on the horizon
When it rises
The sounds of love from her lips and body
Her hair, her eyes, her reassuring voice
Holding hands and slowly walking as we talk
Times of solitude with God
Getting into bed and the way it feels falling asleep
Looking forward to being together again, knowing life is so
tenuous
Saying I love you and knowing it is genuine even when it is not
returned
Praying to the God I know loves us all
Looking out into those stars and feeling that sense of awe and mystery
Speculating about the Creator of it all
Witnessing another April and the feelings of spring
Knowing in my knower God loves me just as I am
Those late light filled summer nights and feeling so warm and
secure
The sensations of my body and soul
Oh these things of life that must be lived to know with
All the painful moments life demands
To feel and say thank You God this gift of life
So real, so perplexing, so impossible to figure out
This gift of life so precious and difficult to let go
To trust to God the right time and place
To do what we can to be helpful and kind
And faith, oh sweet blind faith that all is well
No matter what
To trust, to dream, and to stay serene
Aye God, thank You our precious gift of life…

All
Twisted
Up

All twisted up
sideways
Inside
           Disappointed in everyone
Expectations so HIGH they block the sun
Too serious

Too many judgments
Trembling, how will I ever get out of
This state of mind

Seeing thus
Not enough
Trying to change myself
Is like trying to empty the ocean
Into the sun

I am hoisting the white flag
"I surrender
Please help me
There is never enough
I cannot do this myself
And be even close to
A happy, joyous being"

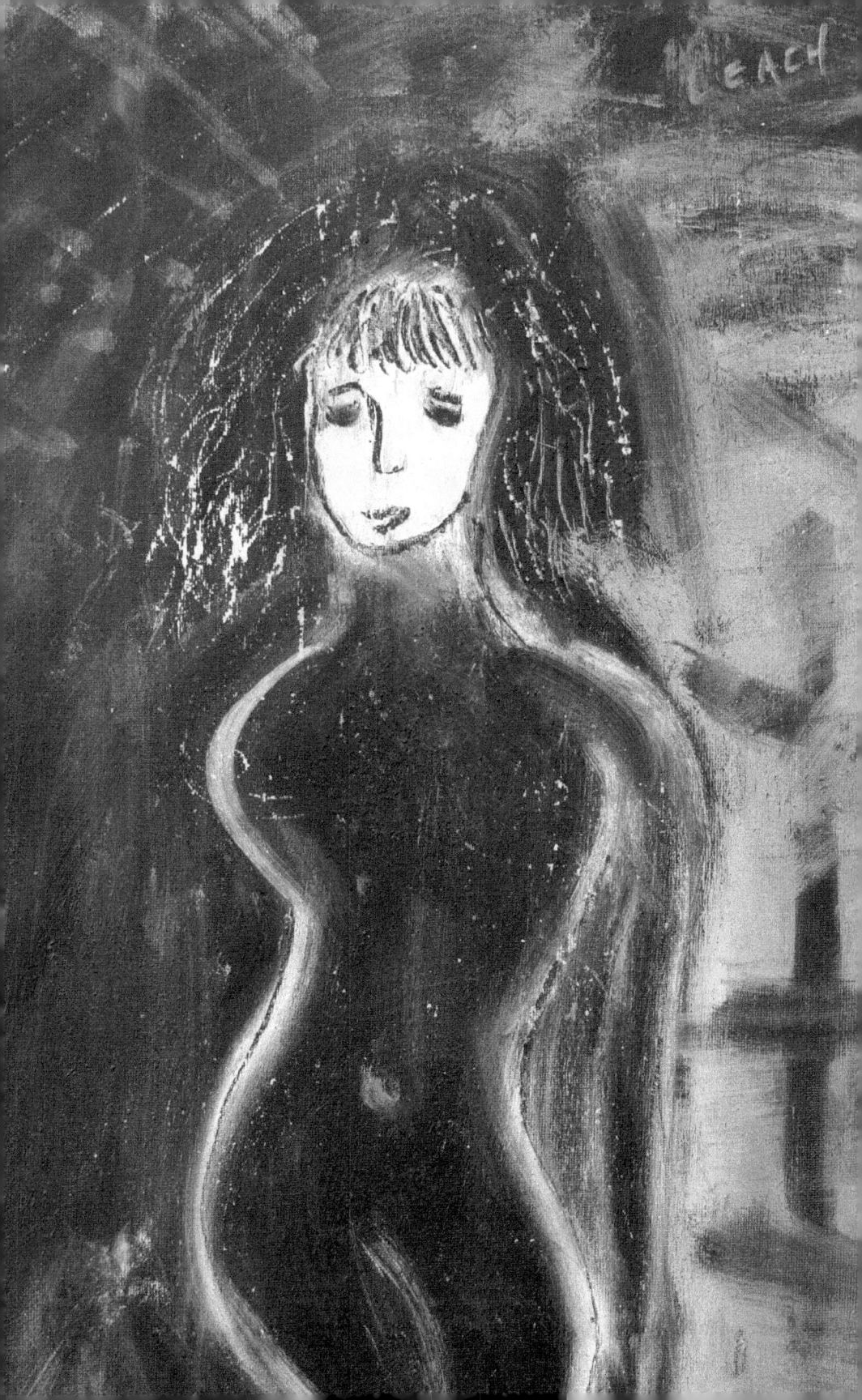

LIVES LIVED

Separately and together
our journeys
through what we call eternity
knowing it is all the same
that nothing lasts forever
and nothing ends that never was

we believe so little
so obvious we do not see
or believe in what we see
with eyes closed
our teeth clenched
fearing we will
die too soon
or live too long
in pain
or not have enough
or have too much
or die without knowing
why we were here

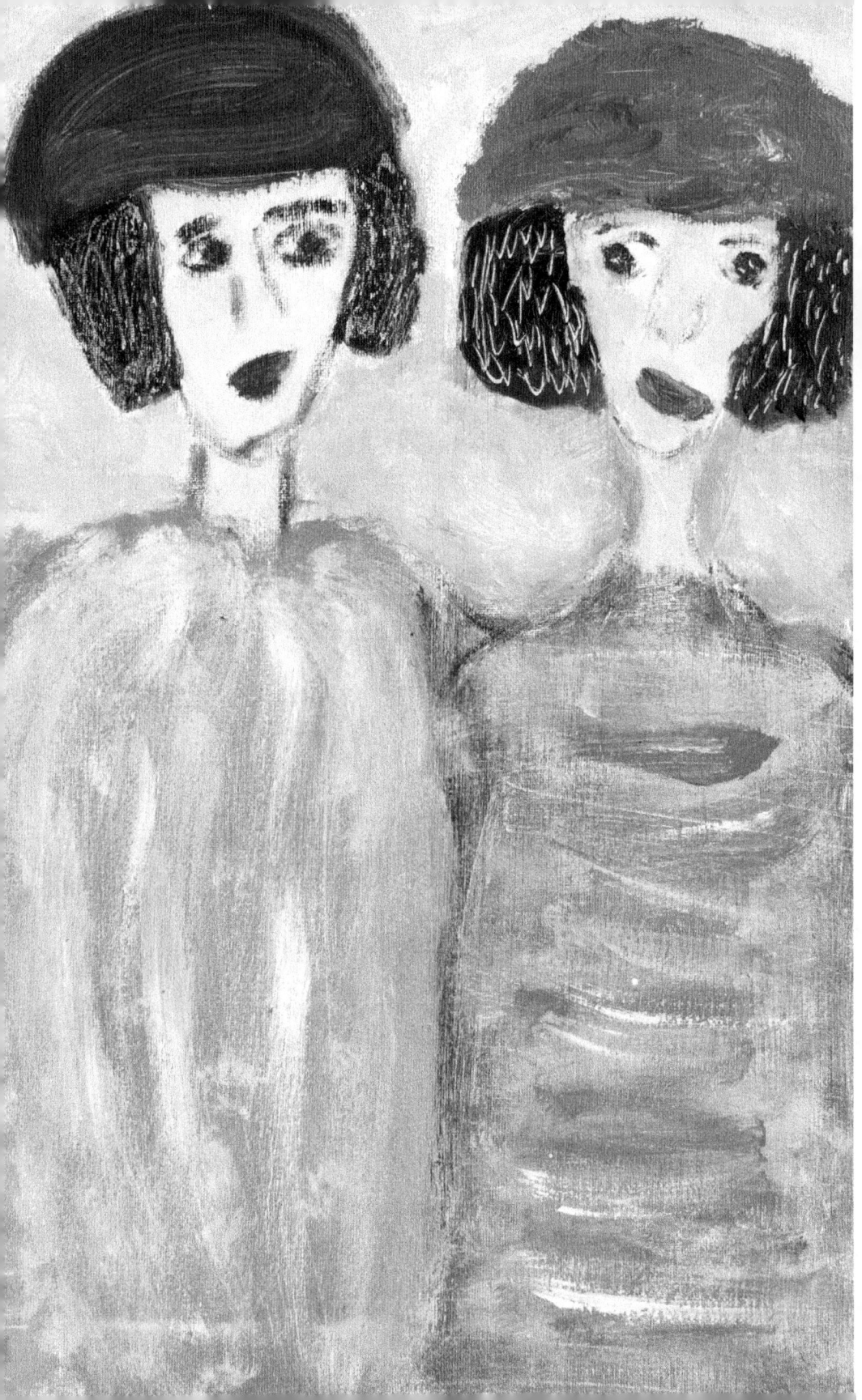

My Truth

I have never been a very popular person
people do not seem very interested in me or what
I have to offer, do not seek me out often
so my telephone does not ring much and I
am not invited out to many social events.

And I cannot figure out what it is that turns people
away. I try to be kind, and show respect, and be
a good man. This seeming aversion to me
applies to both men and women.

What I fear is that people avoid me because
they know in my heart I cannot truly love them
and am selfish even when I am trying to be
kind and generous. Without divine intervention
I am afraid I will not be able to change.

Now at 53 years old I feel a need to accept life
as life is and be grateful for the good friends I do
have, people I try to appreciate and rejoice with
in our friendship. I pray God for your help and
guidance being the man you would have me be
and quietly accept the facts of life as they are.

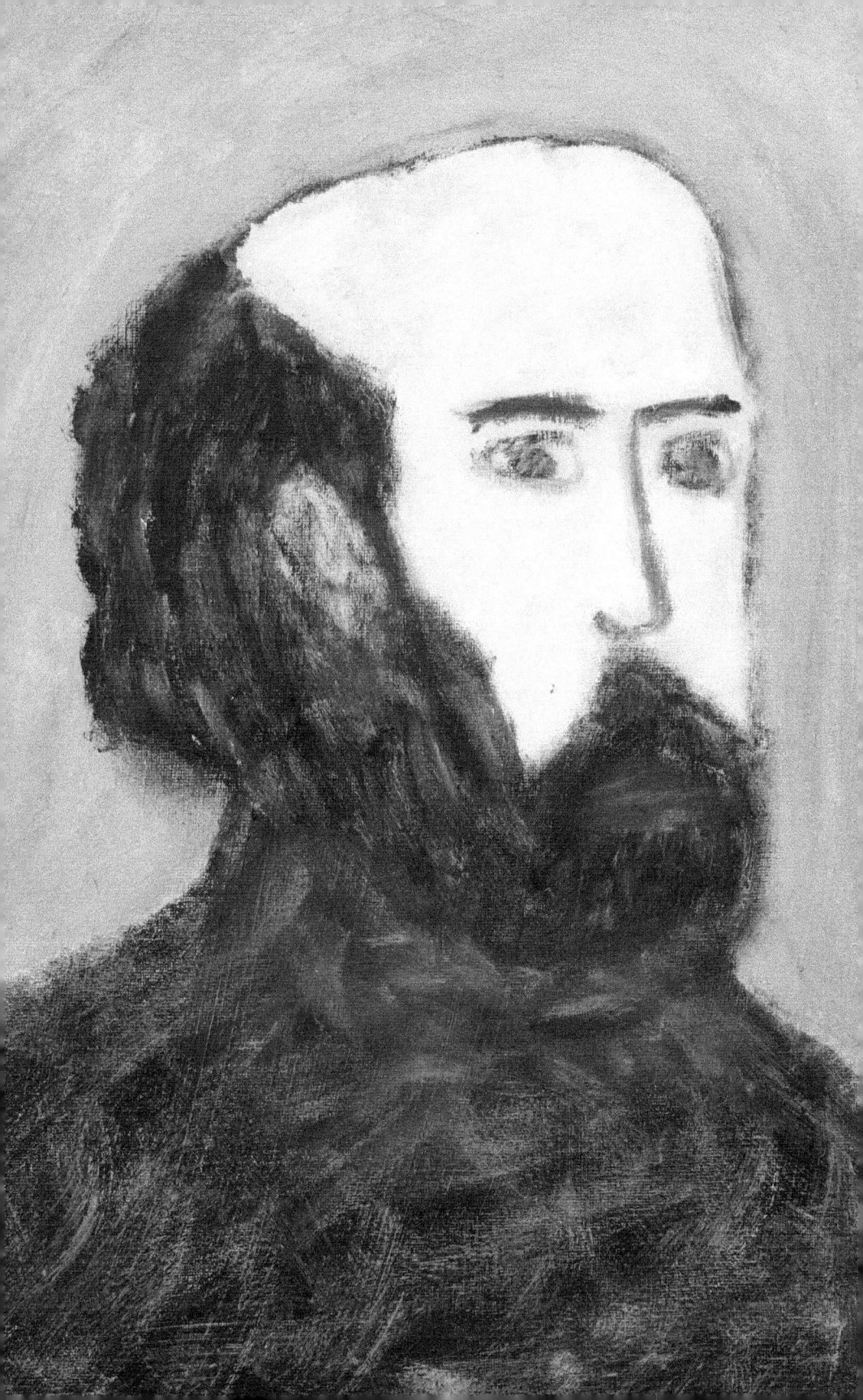

SAVING FOR ETERNITY
(Horrible Dreams of Passion and Remorse)

Cedar walls encompass
This sad house
The loneliness
The integrity forsaken for self defense

Living life's journey as though
Saving for eternity
Struggling with indigo waves
Of spontaneity glaring on like
The full moon's emotionless stare

Buffalo dreams and broken families
Of taverns to pain
Of branching green-blue flower tops distain
Substances that feel good killing slowly
Our precious lives spent
Fleeing the insanity within
With violent fluids chilled on
Iced down emotions

Does anyone still believe
In kindness
In friendship
In my sojourn with courage
In the integrity of unaltered feelings?

Our sands of time spread
With children's toys
With weapons and bank accounts
Living and dying and disintegrating
Stranding aging life forms in time

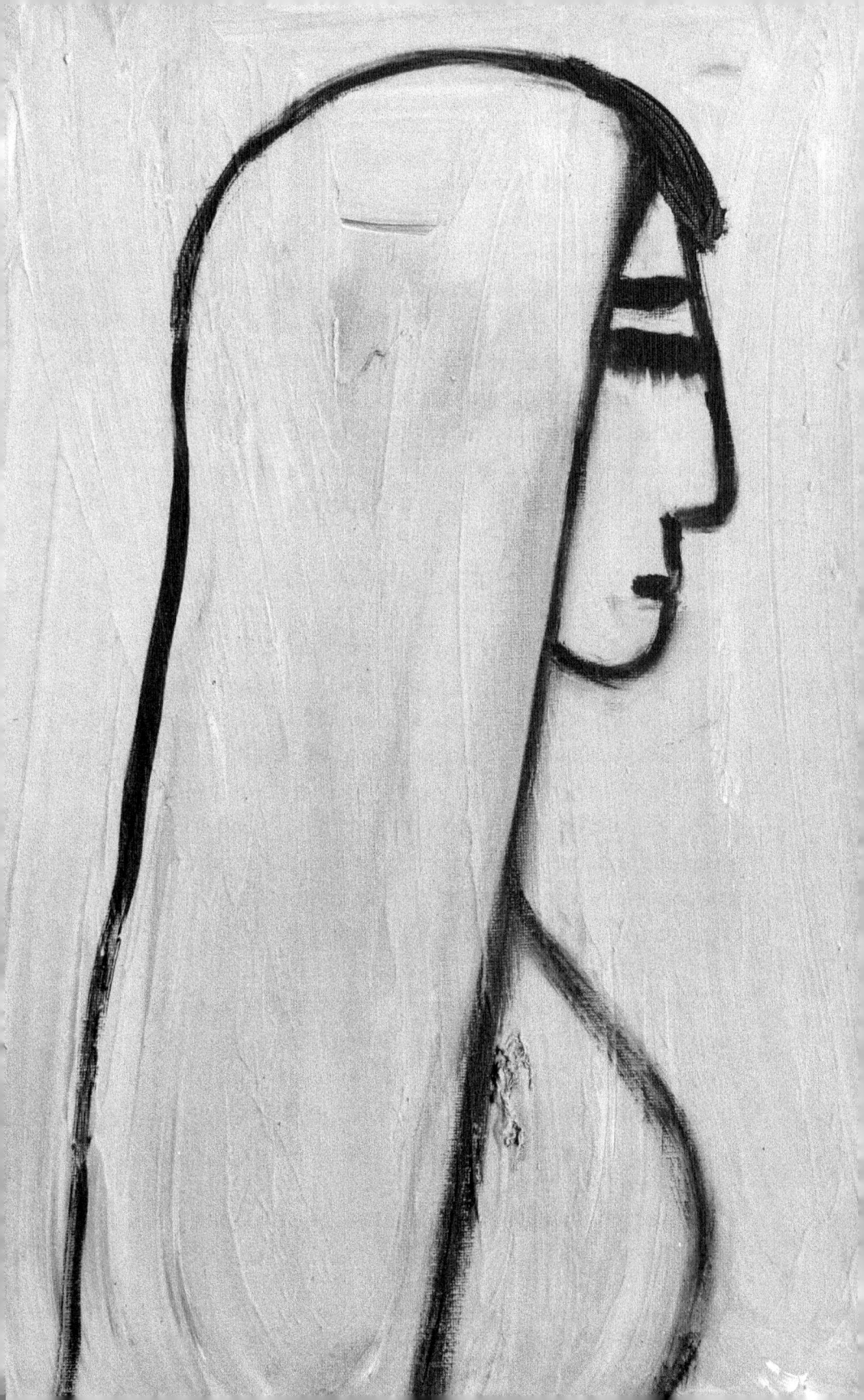

God

A friend asked me to write about my concept of spirituality. I responded that God is a mystery I rely on and offer myself to, a presence in my life I pray to and meditate with and ask for faith and trust in. More needs to be said.

I feel God in my soul, I know I am part of God and God is part of me and you and everyone, all living beings everywhere, plants and animals and insects, everyone, on this planet and other places we don't know about yet. I know this in my knower, but I do not know how to define what it is or is not. My life is a mystery, why I am here or what I am supposed to do a mystery so I ask God to help me with all that, knowing I'm probably doing a very imperfect job but knowing God loves me anyway. I want to tell her I trust that God will know what to do with me when I die and that I do not need to fear God anymore because I know God would not harm me no matter what. It is we who harm ourselves and each other saying it is God. God would never hurt us.

So God, I reach into you praying way deep inside, please help me do what I was sent here to do, whether it is to write this or paint our next painting or take the next breath, I ask only that we do it together one moment at a time. There is so much good in the human soul despite all the bad in us, our music, our art, our literature and poetry, our love, our kindness, our compassion, our many forms of reaching out to our divine mystery we call God in so many different languages and images, we need You now more than ever as we grope our way along so blind to the effects of our actions on this little planet in this vast universe. And that's the best I can do trying to explain my concept of relationship with God other than to say God gives my life meaning and purpose and hope and gratitude to be alive.

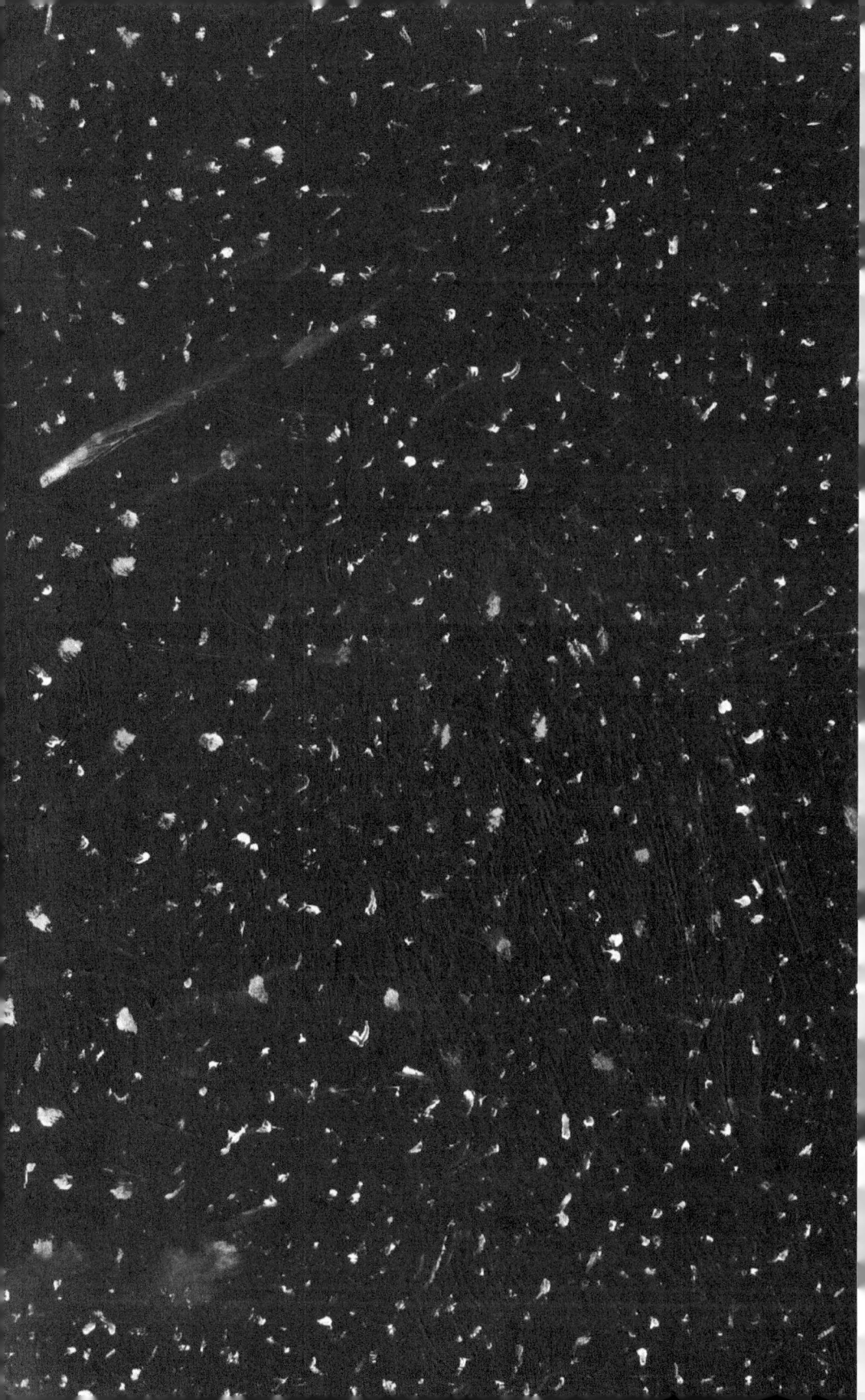

THE TROUBLE WITH TRYING TO LIVE WITHOUT GOD

The trouble with trying to live without God
is that life is a lonely struggle with me in charge

I need God in my life, a personal relationship not with
God as other people talk about God but as I learn to be with
God

I turn to that mysterious Presence within and pray for faith, not
a strength which comes naturally to me

Resting finally with prayers for God to be in charge of
everything
For me this was not always so and I burned in an emotional

desert of my own making trying to wrest all the hedonistic
pleasures possible out of life only to find myself suicidal,

spiritually bankrupt, and more miserable than I'd ever dreamed
possible. In desperation I asked God for help, the God I'd

abandoned decades ago, being the educated, scientific, show
me kind of intelligent man I thought I was and God helped me

and helps me every day, so long as I am willing to try to live
the way I believe God wants me to live. The trouble with

trying to live without God is that life becomes so lonely and
personal and empty with that huge hollowness within

that only belief in a spiritual presence greater than myself
can begin to fill and make whole . . .

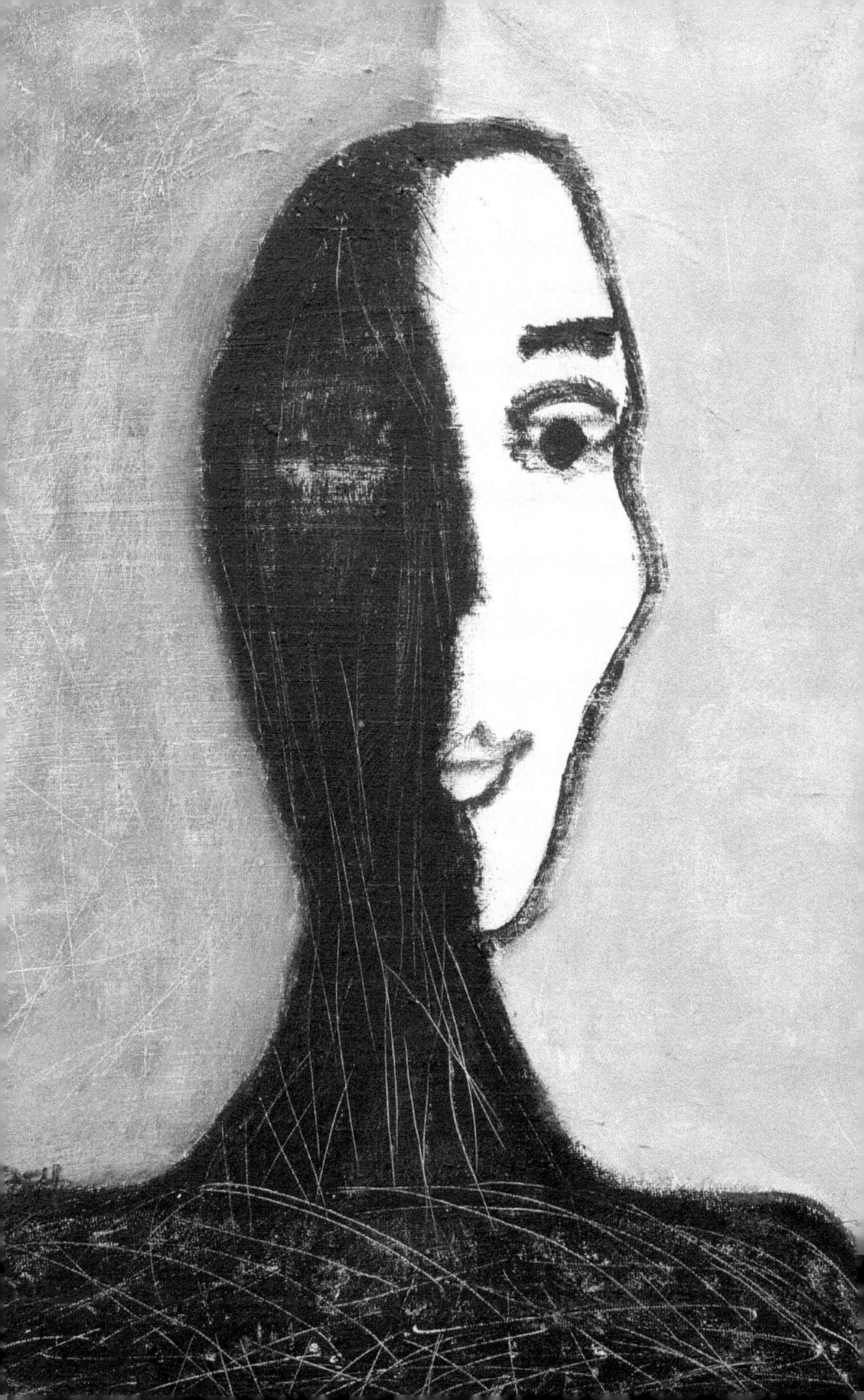

Someone Cut A Hole In My Head

Someone cut a hole in my head
Took out my self-confidence
My faith that I am worthy of love and self-respect
I do not know how to get it back
That big hole inside my head
Perhaps this is my lot in life
Just when I thought I was getting well

II
it comes and goes
waxes and wanes
tidal shift high and low and in between
never steady and exact

so who allowed the low tide to fool me again?
the ocean is on its way back
there are holes in my head
Patience
self-confidence is coming back

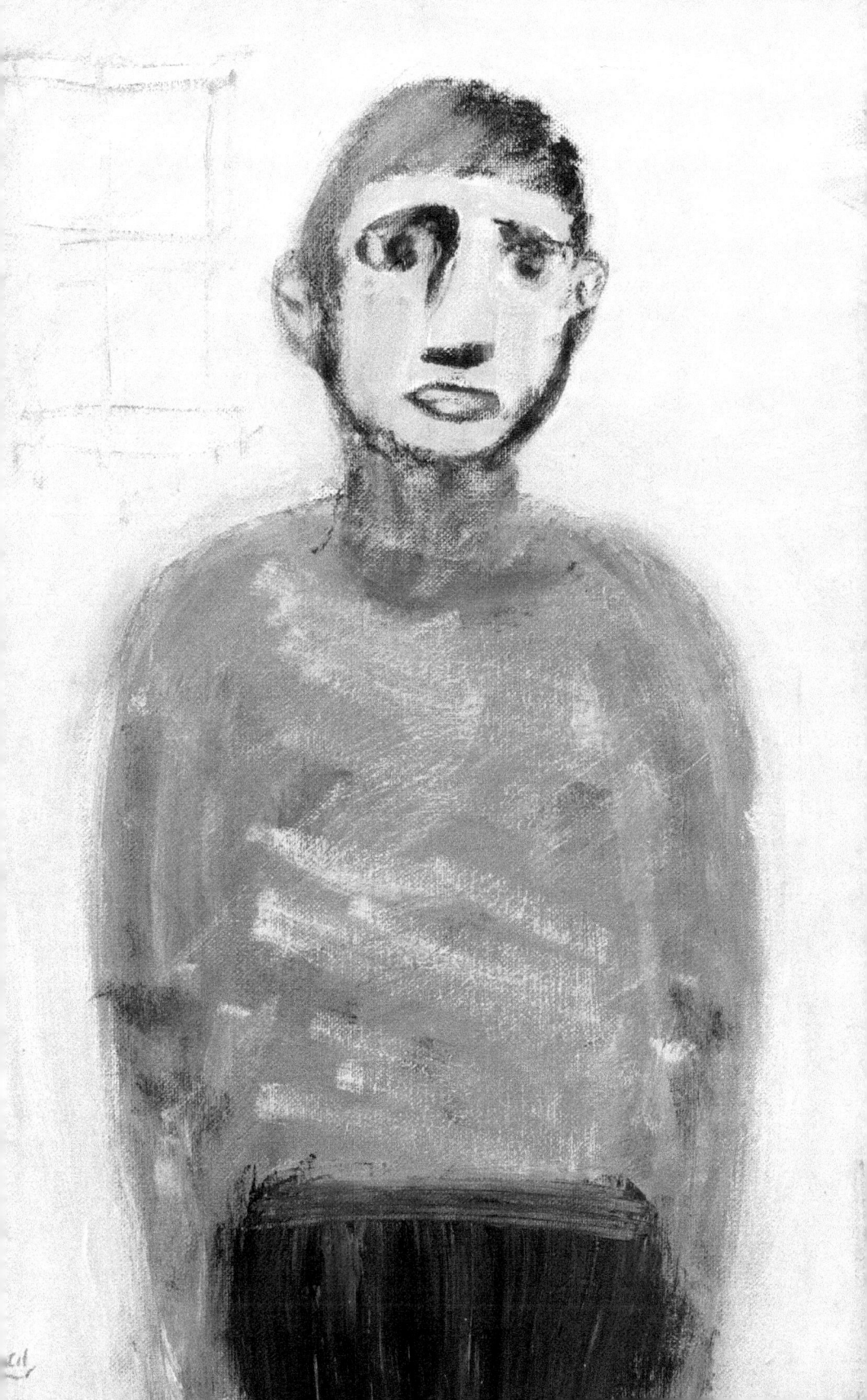

Sitting In The Tree of Life with God Holding Me

I

I went to federal prison to visit men locked away
inside, met bank robbers, pot growers, thieves and many whose
crimes I'll never know

Ten years with no parole and there's no way out till you've
served your time

The prison culture I do not understand, how could I
survive inside?

So grateful when the time was up I could leave, walk
outside and drive away
My crimes go unpunished
Sitting in the tree of life with God
Celebrating, I am free
Almost two decades since I've committed a crime
minor as they may be in my own mind; I met men who were there
who did not seem very different from me

II

God speaks through wind blowing in the trees
Sun spreading light and warmth, a life force making leaves green
and alive
God touches us with rain and rivers and lakes and ocean waves
God lives in all beings and things
Sitting in the tree of life with the squirrels and birds and insects
and bees saying "I love you just the way you are"

III

Sitting in the tree of life with God asking "Why me, why here on this
planet, why now? What am I here to do, what would you have me be?"
And the wind whispering for God:
"Enjoy life with me, that's all I ask of anyone or anything"

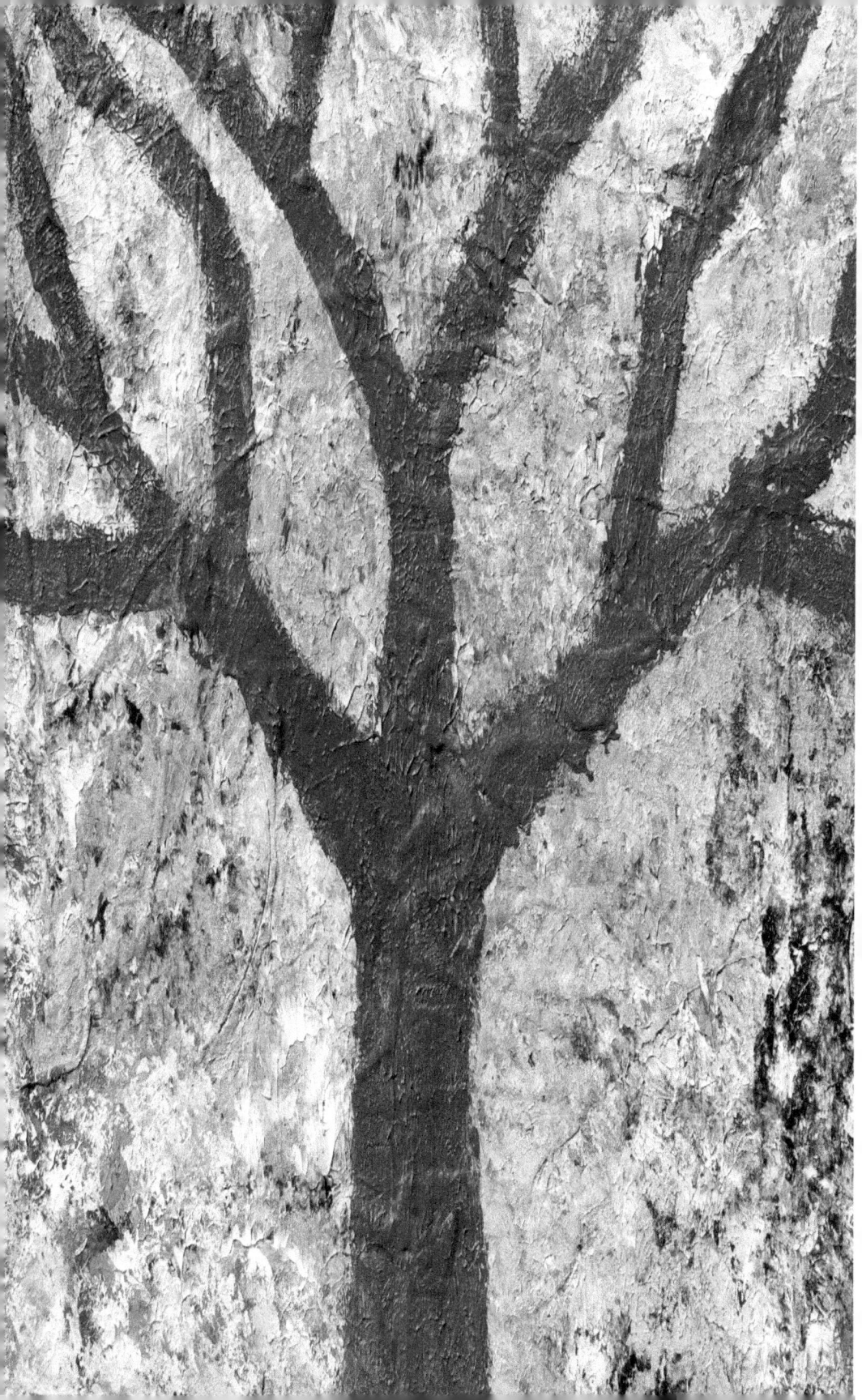

DEATH

My first encounter with death was when my paternal grandfather got cancer and died after months of suffering in a nursing home. I was about 10 when he died.

I remember looking at other kids playing across from the funeral parlor wondering how they could be so happy on such a sad, sad day, like ours was the only family that had a loss so great.

My grandfather always looked old to me, with the smell of whiskey on his breath and dark brown Seagrams 7 bottles in his hand. The man who delighted at throwing a pocketful of coins on the living room floor and watching my brother and I scramble to get them, shouting words of competition and laughing at us. The man who would periodically quit drinking for brief periods and then complain about my grandmother's alcohol problem. The man who would insist on giving me hot water bottle enemas out of a small pouch with a long hose and nozzle, giving me candy to make it alright. I learned to never complain about a stomach ache to him.

Truth is I never knew the man well, but I mourned his passing because everyone else did and he would be missed, so we said. The man who fathered the alcoholic egomaniac monster I knew as my father.

Since his passing I've lost all my other grandparents, my aunts, my father, my mother, and with time I've learned some measure of forgiveness. I've experienced my alcoholism and my attempt to invite death early to end my life, so grateful now death declined and Life prevailed.

Death comes to us all, and I pray for peace with death when it comes, and a meaningful life well lived until then…

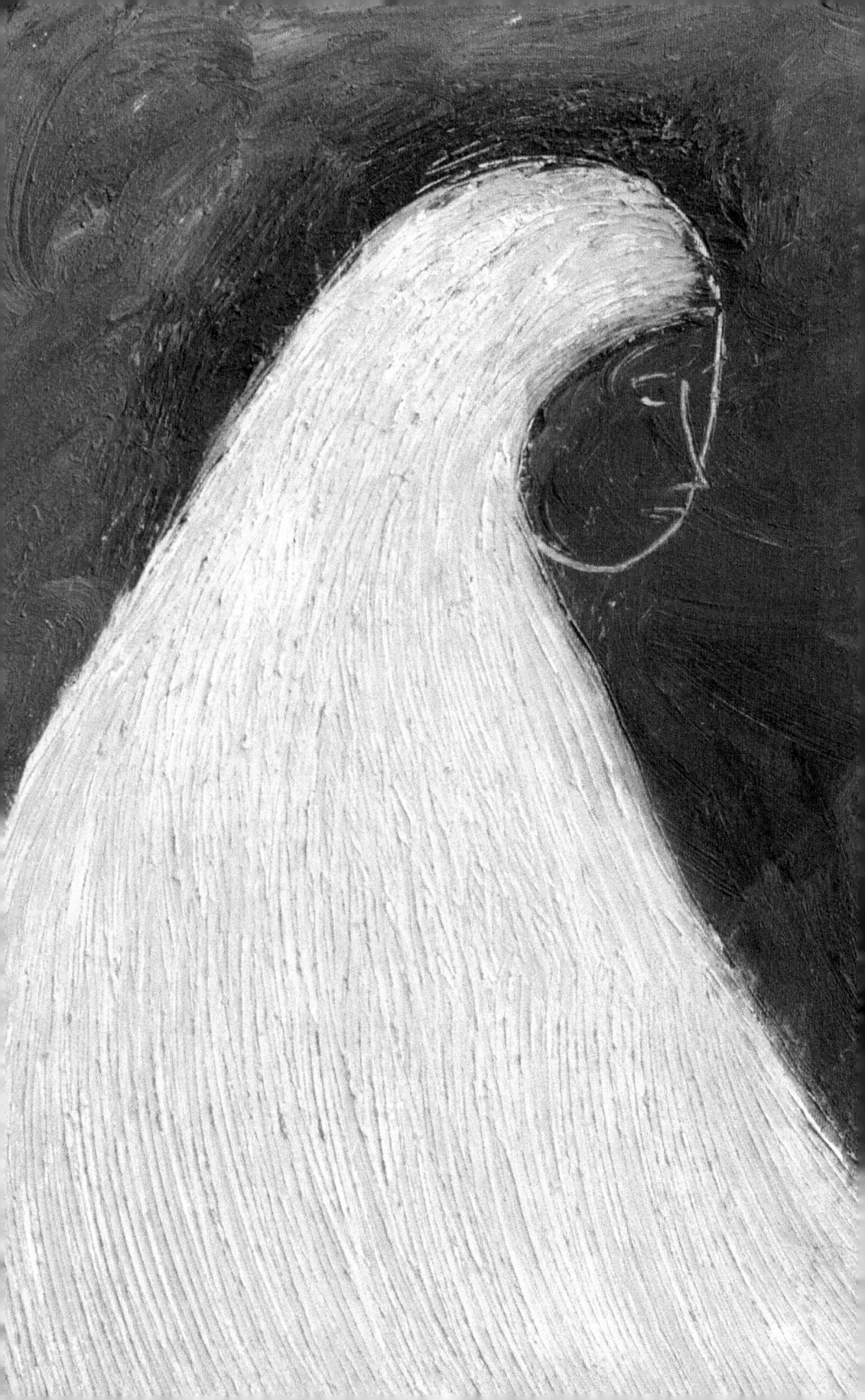

The Little Voice

Gossamer strands in the air
Tonight, the sun is going down
It chased me all day long, calling
Out, asking me to take time off and play
Or sit a while, relax, enjoy the
Final days of summer here
But I said no, refused to play "I've
Work today, so behind before I start"
Ran from the sun and hid in the shade to work

**

There is a still small voice inside my
Head that talks to me in silent words
Advises me, do this, not that
Call it what you will, you know it well, I believe, just like me

My life goes so much smoother when I heed the still small
voice inside my head
So often I've gone the opposite way and paid the price
Because it is my life, or is it shared with God who created me

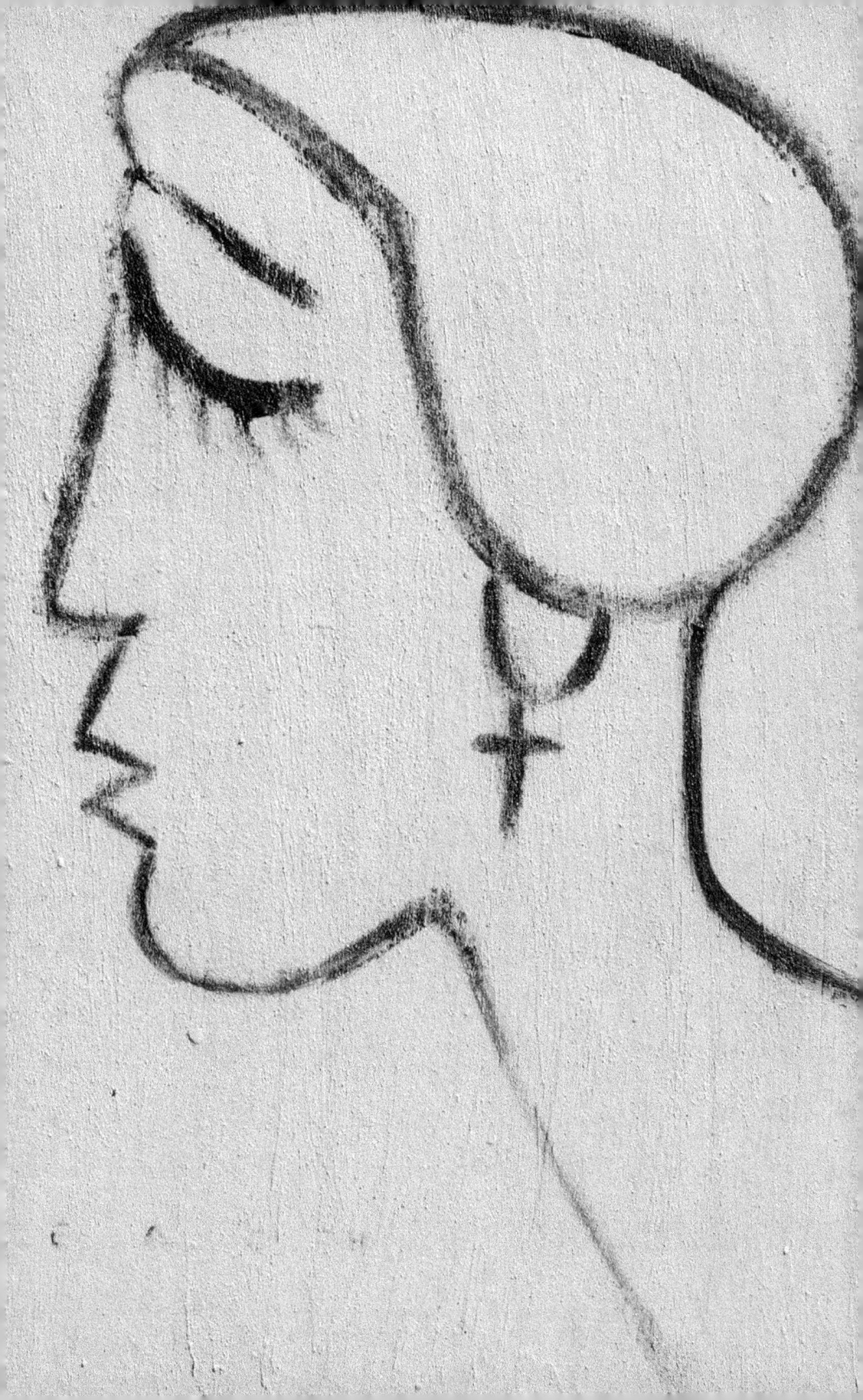

LONELINESS

has been my companion for most
of my life, even when I lived with
women who loved me, and family
and friends. In my experience I
see tremendous value in solitude
with God, balanced with work
and relationships with friends.

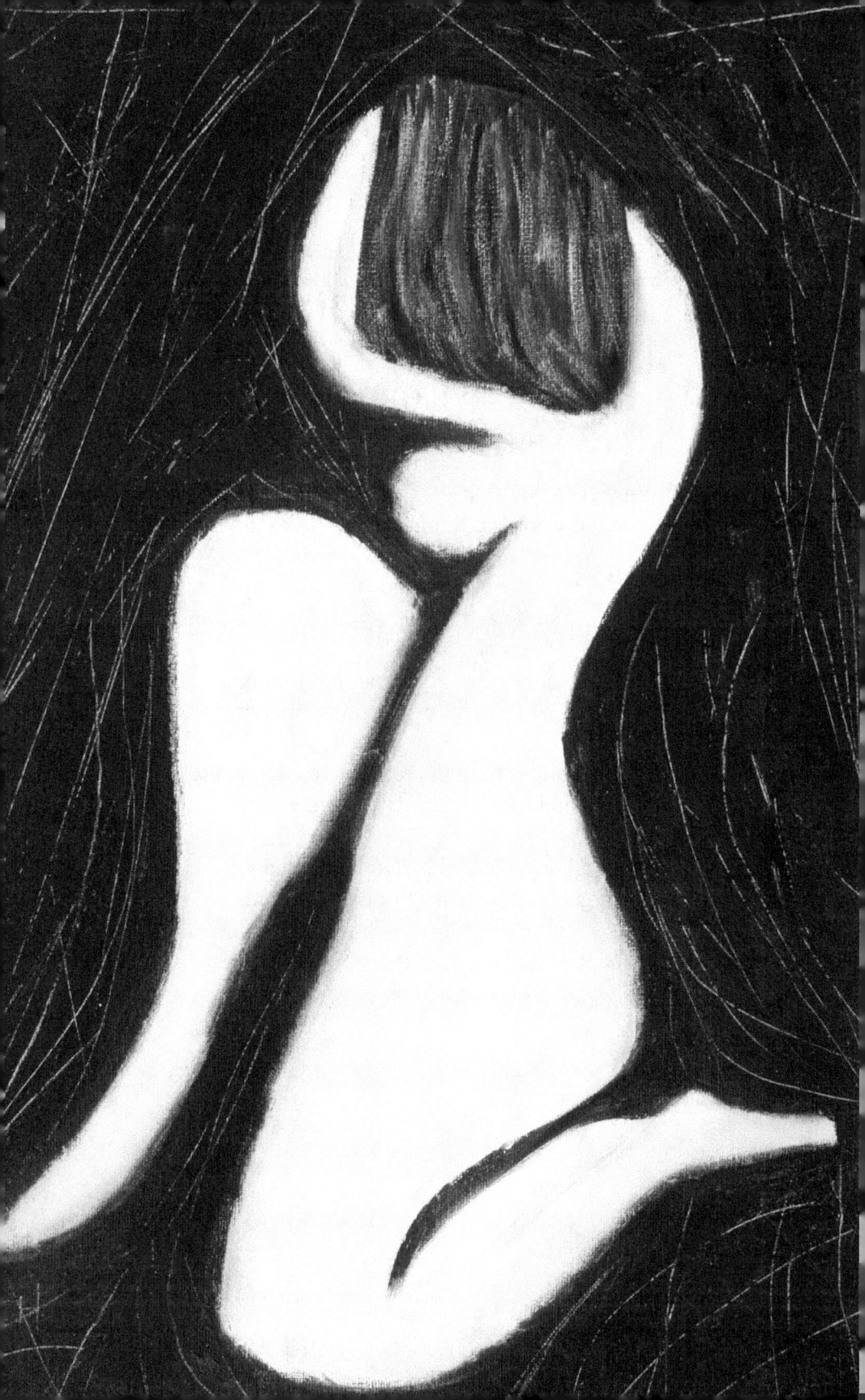

ABOVE GROUND

Whenever I'd ask him
"Len, how are you doing today," he would say

"Pat, any day above ground is a good day."
And he'd smile and shake my hand, every time.

Len's no longer above ground, but I think about
him often when I feel in one of my moods.

Len and I were both in recovery from a deadly
disease, and I feel every day above ground

Is a good day, blessed by God, a sacred gift
we all get to experience through good times

And not so good, a sacred gift for each of us,
this mystery of being alive.

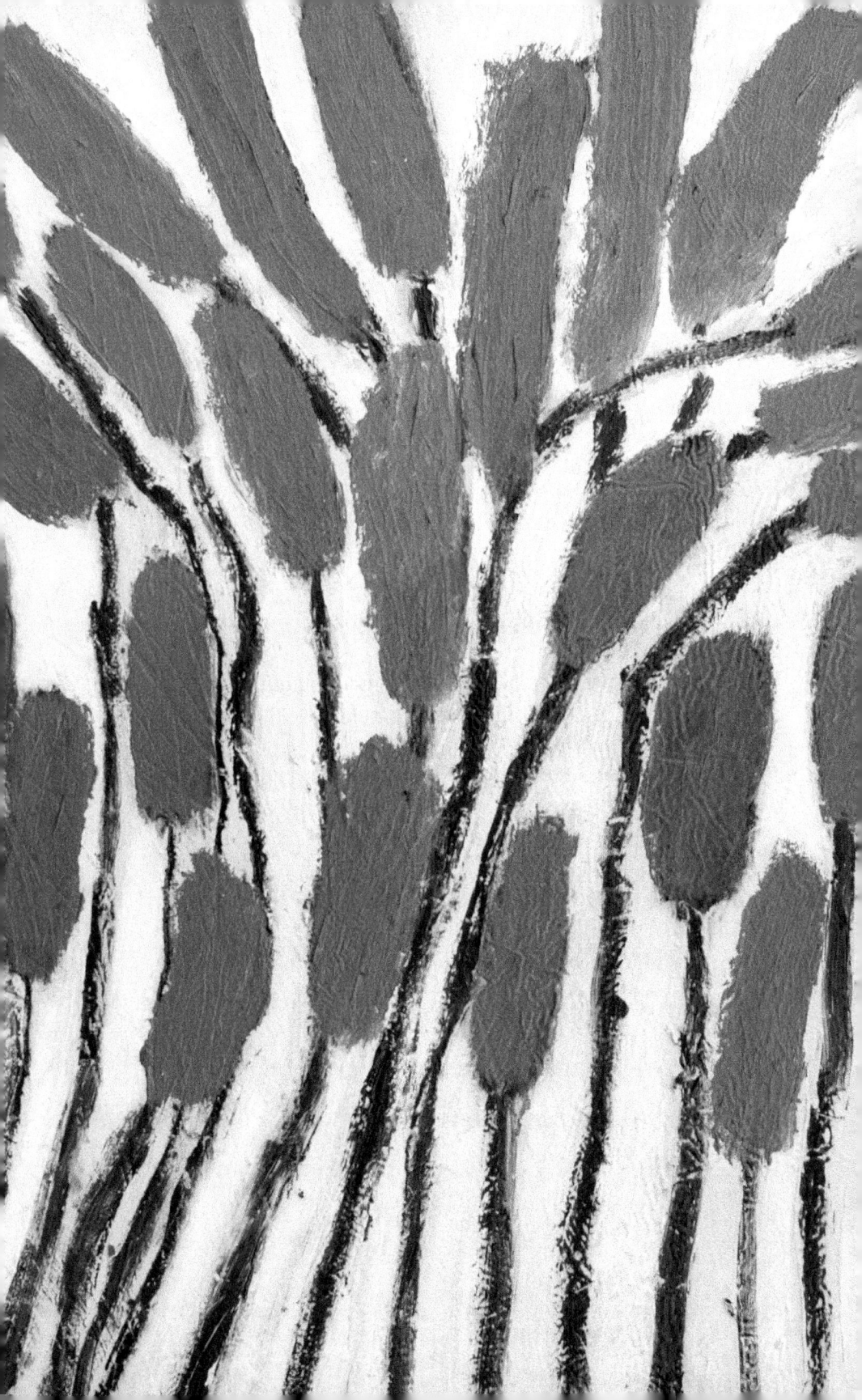

A Man

Has no better or worse way to live
Than when he tries his best

So often this man muddles through
His life not trusting that life is happening exactly

As it is meant to happen and that all he has to do
Is relax and work in harmony and enjoy the journey

Take some risks by enjoying himself and doing what
He feels drawn to do even though it may not be the

Most conservative or logical, lucrative, or socially
acceptable, but it is the path he will thrive on

If he trusts the universe to care for and nurture him
In the best possible ways

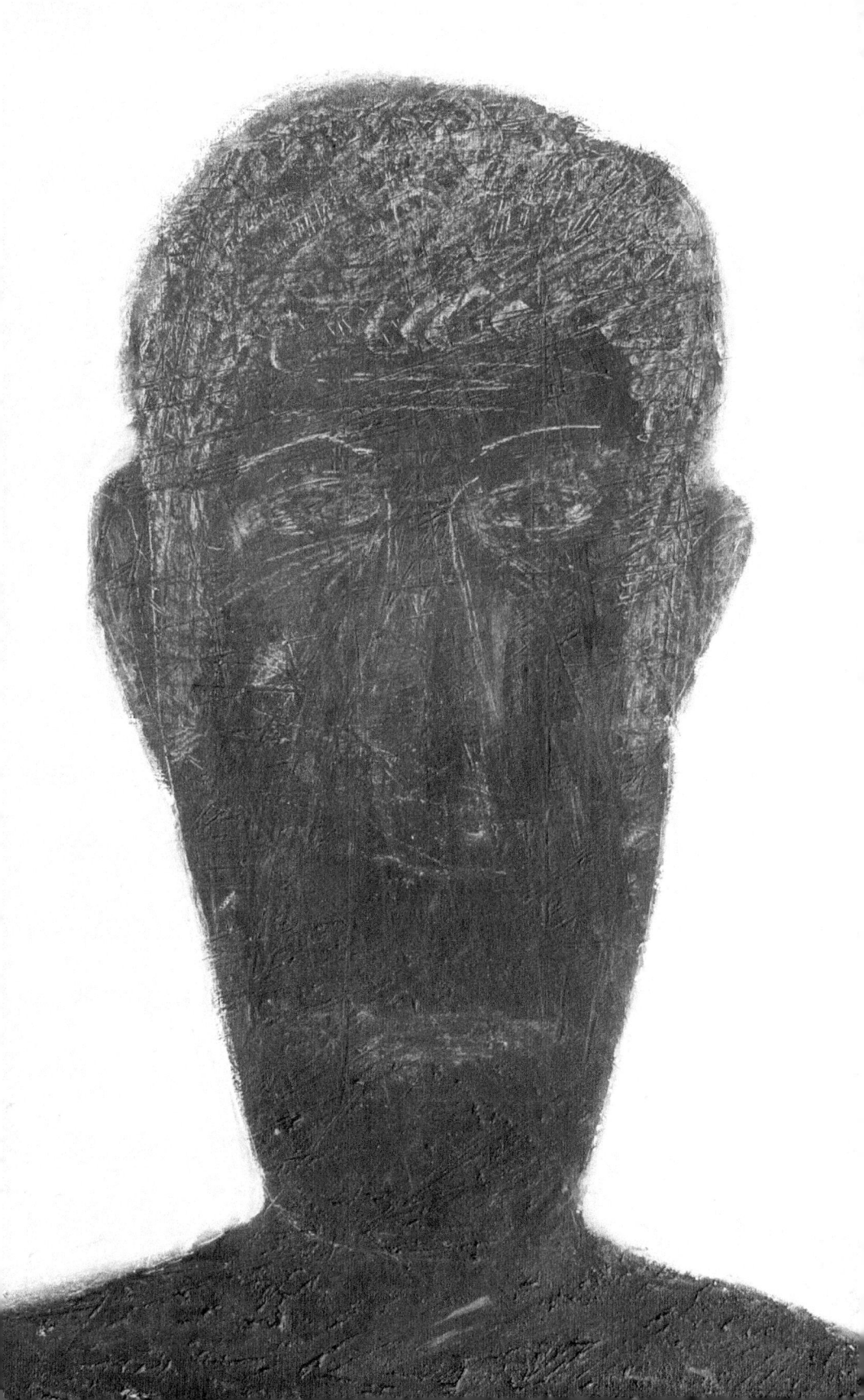

Three Men

Three men in recovery
Talking 2 hours about what is eating away at them
From within, each with their own set of problems
To talk out

One his work relationships, a good white collar job
With powerful, feminist women
And his diversions into offending
Wondering what is good and healthy for him

Another his broken relationship with the woman
He loved
Their fighting, pointing fingers, accusing
Her leaving when it got bad enough, his pain and
Loneliness another good relationship gone bad

The third his current relationship
The ups and the downs weathering years now
Healthy and vibrant overall
His questions about the nature of love
Needing independence, boundaries
Questioning if he is willing to give her enough
To stay

It felt so good to be part of this group
Wanting to do this again
Without judging, knowing there is something
Genuine and honest shared in this group
Our relationships and lack of them
Are often what troubles us the most

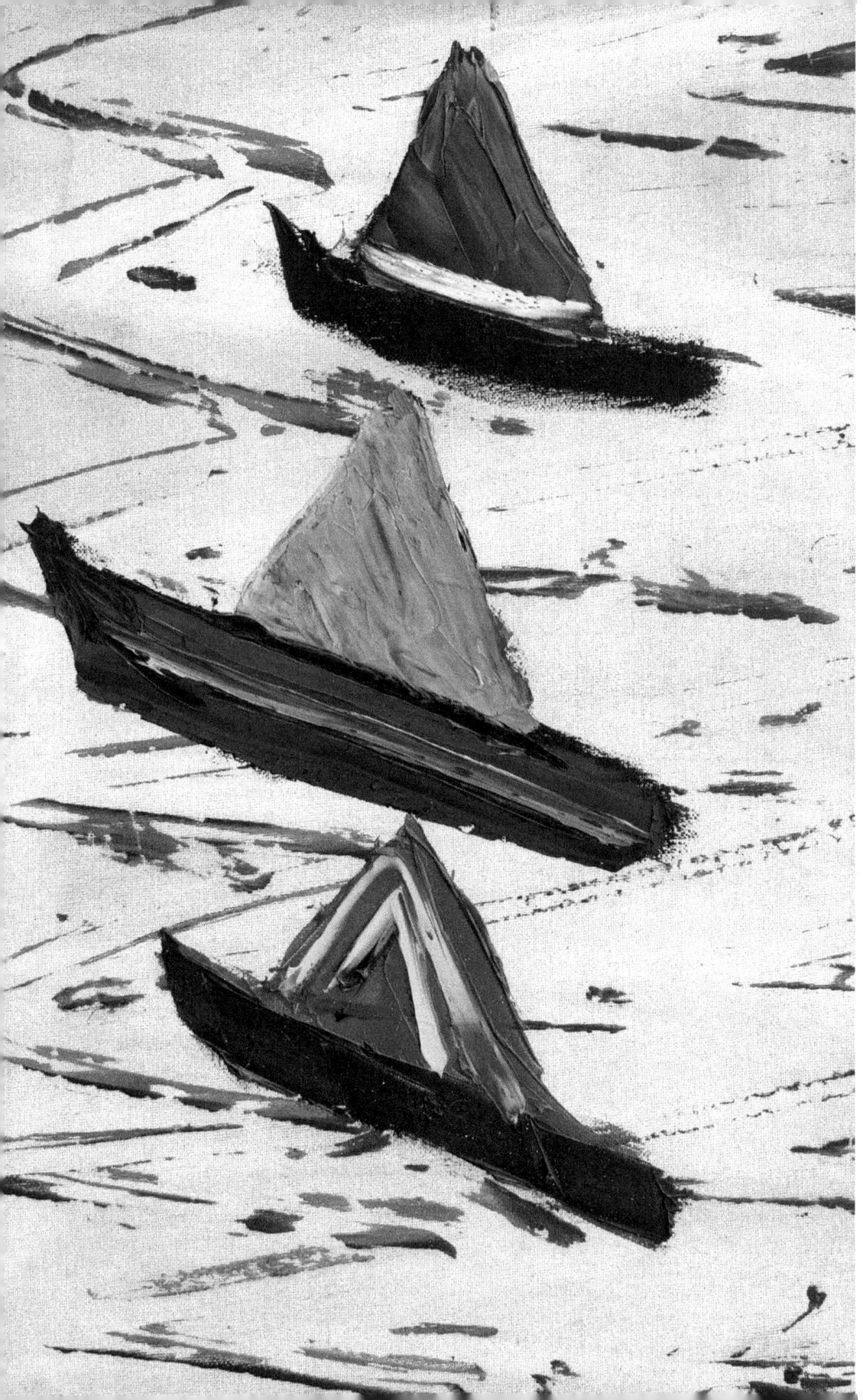

Now

Thank you God
this poem
these feelings
this sober
life
here
with
You

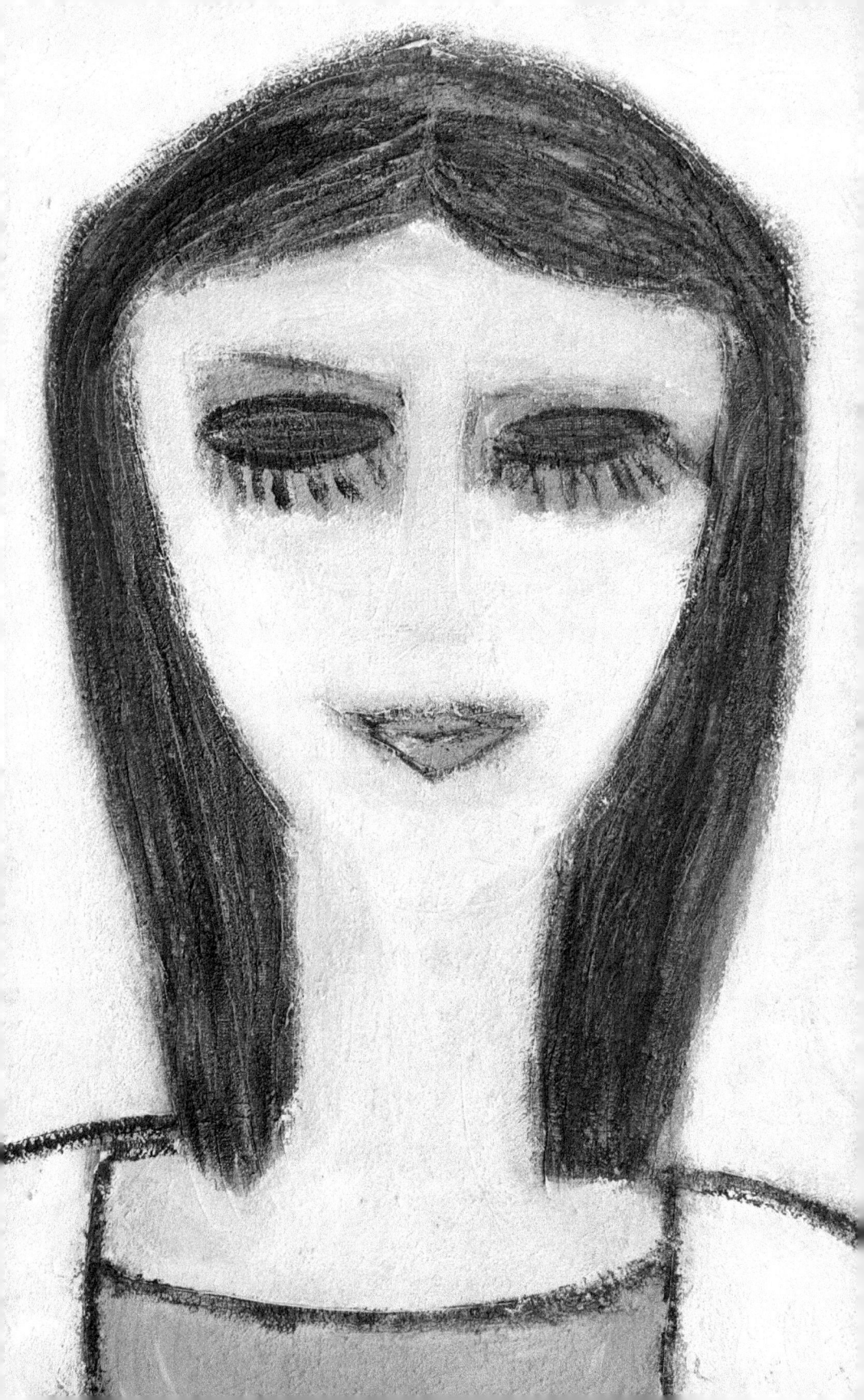

It Snowed Last Night

White snowflakes came visiting

Last night, water in crystalline form

Sunshine through clouds visits now

Nice to look out at it all

From this warm comfortable spot

In the world I call home

Such a beautiful changing scene

Closer now to spring

Hoping the crocus and daffodils

Don't get too cold to bloom

Someday I'd like to follow

North to south back north

Two times a year to spring

Feeling grateful to be here now

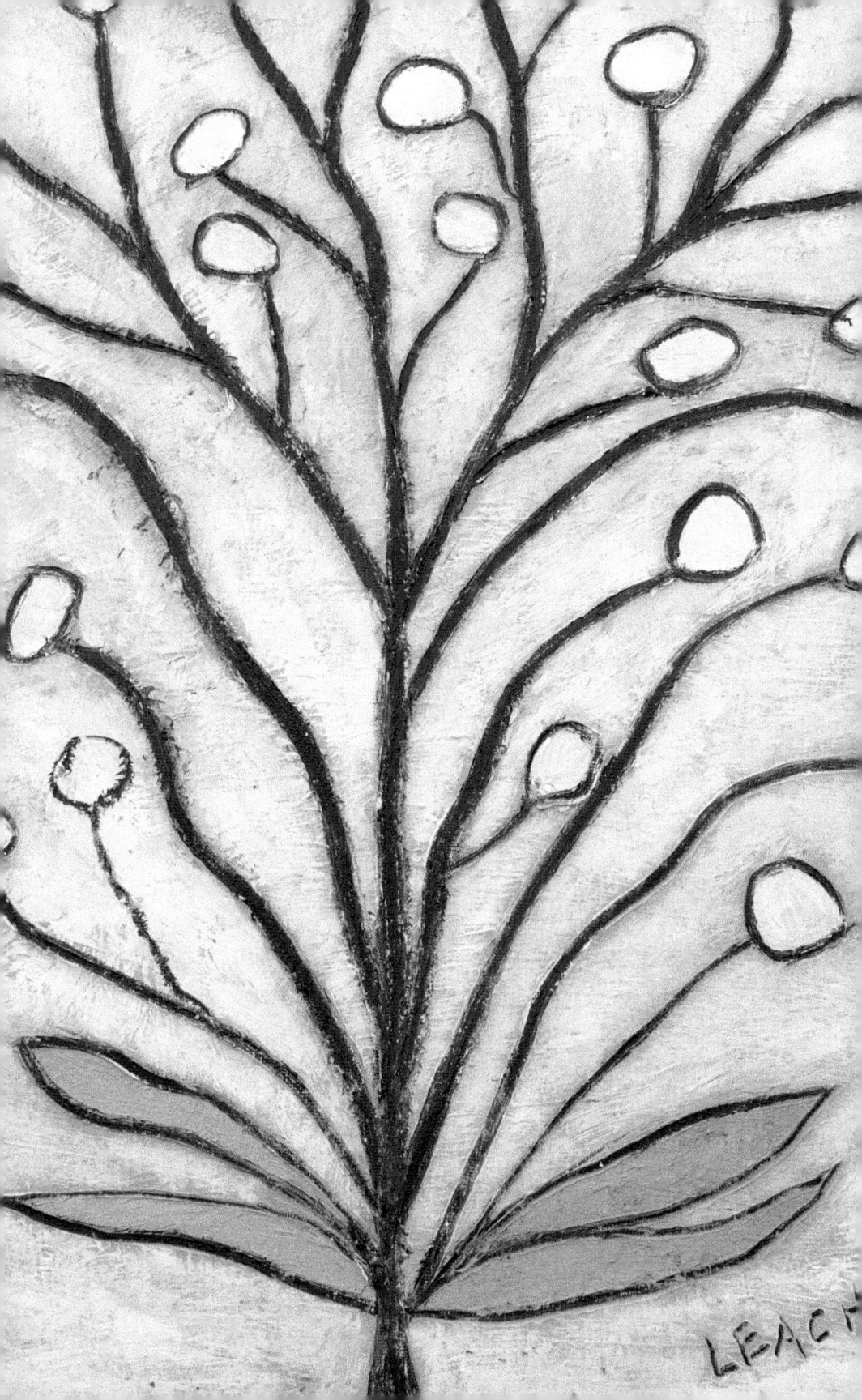

MY ALCOHOLISM

Coming to next day wondering how I hurt myself, again
with the big black and blue mark on my body to the bone
not remembering anything past a certain point

How those blackouts became so commonplace
so dreaded were those out of control times
not knowing how I got home or what happened
avoiding people I'd called at two in the morning
and realizing they too were avoiding me

Losing control of my behavior and morality
those escort services and wasted money
my stolen MasterCard after I'd passed out
and the bills I'd not charged
the loneliness and confusion, the desperation
and broken relationships

Thinking I'd somehow figure out how to drink in a
controlled way as my alcoholism progressed and had
its way with me and those around me
trying to control the uncontrollable

Doing questionable things to make money
as I could not hold down a job
the disgust and terror I felt being so out of control
as my mind desperately sought a way out
with death by suicide making more and more sense

Thank You God and people in recovery for showing me
the way out of my alcoholism and a new
and better life truly worth living

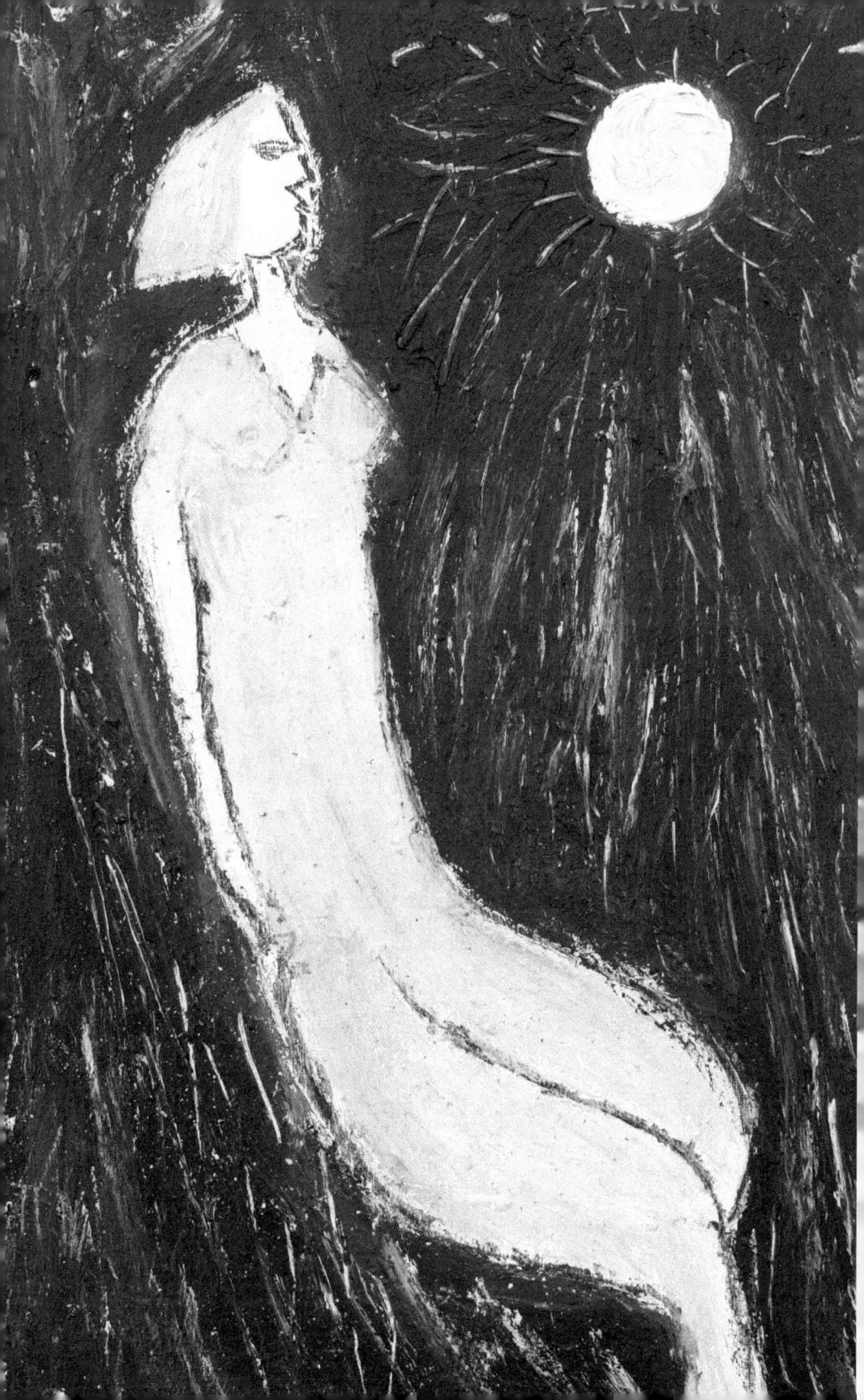

The Silence of Miranda Gwent

A long-haired slender woman, aging gracefully
Educated, artistic, you'd never guess her past

Convicted twice, at 18 and 22, for prostitution,
Incarcerated at 23 for prostitution and grand larceny,
At 24 for drug dealing and grand theft

Mouth like a sewer rat back in the day, drug addicted,
Alcoholic, everyone thought Miranda Gwent would
Be dead before she reached 30

Serving 3 to 5 at the state prison farm for assault with
Intent to kill, Miranda met Shirley Harman, a 47 year
Old chaplain with a criminal past a mile long

And something changed: long talks, rehabilitation,
Meditation, a new relationship with God, a GED, college
Prep, a whole new life began leading years later to a
PhD, writing and lecture career, and helping young women
Turn their lives around like she did way back when

Miranda Gwent does not say much, but when she talks
People listen, they know she loves them unconditionally,
No matter what, she understands all the troubles they face
And genuinely tries to help

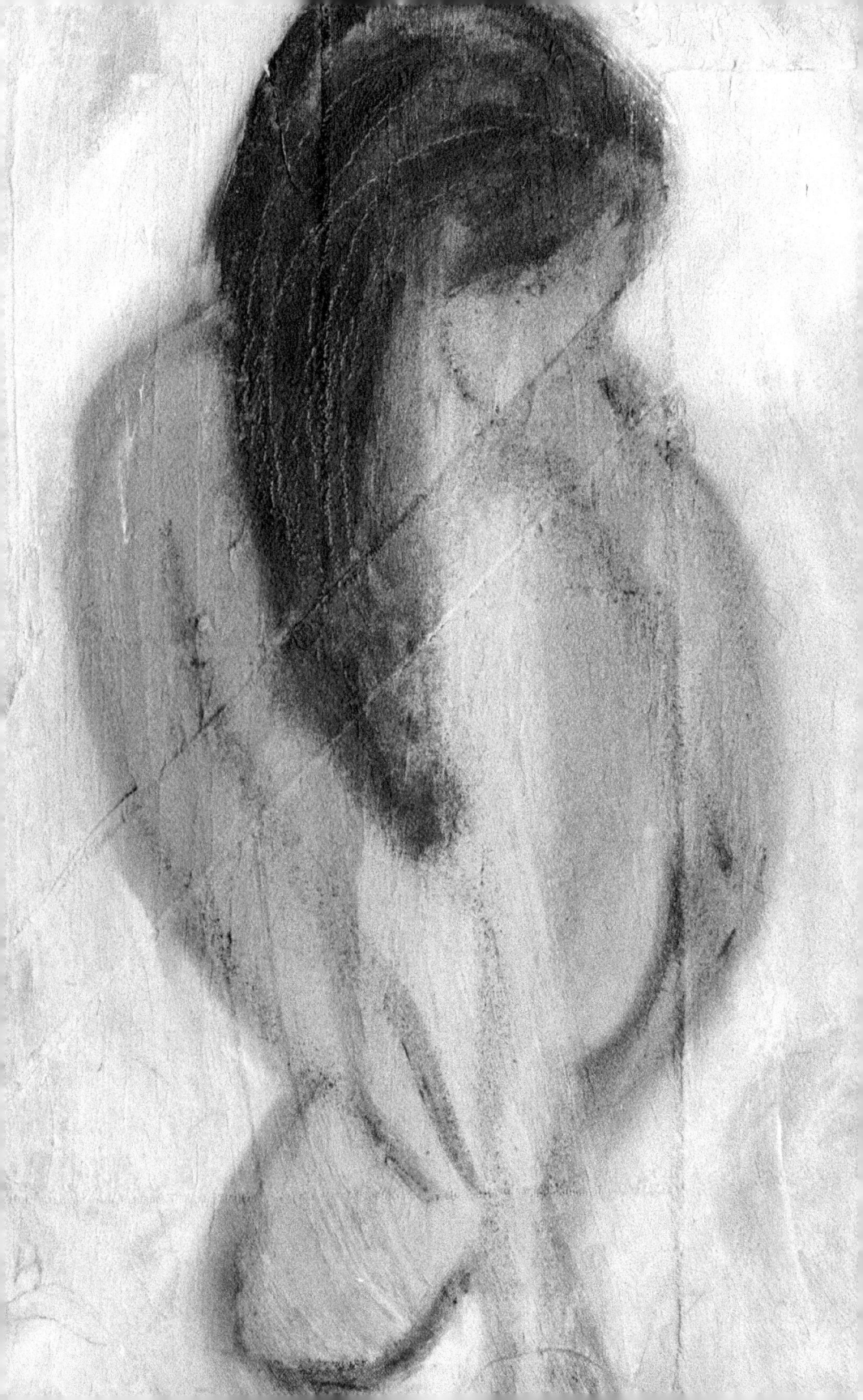

**EASY
DOES
IT**

what happens here
is God's will

    decisions made
    actions taken
    effect the course
    this life takes

    Praying now
    for guidance
    help
    right action,
    forgiveness
    when
    I do wrong

Getting Older

Fear not getting older
the best years of my life
began in my mid 40's
better yet throughout my 50's
and now at 60 I am more
comfortable in my being
this well of spirit
drawing on resources
hitherto unrecognized
surfacing, massaging
in, growing deeper into
the man I am meant to be;
it is taking so long for me
to be me

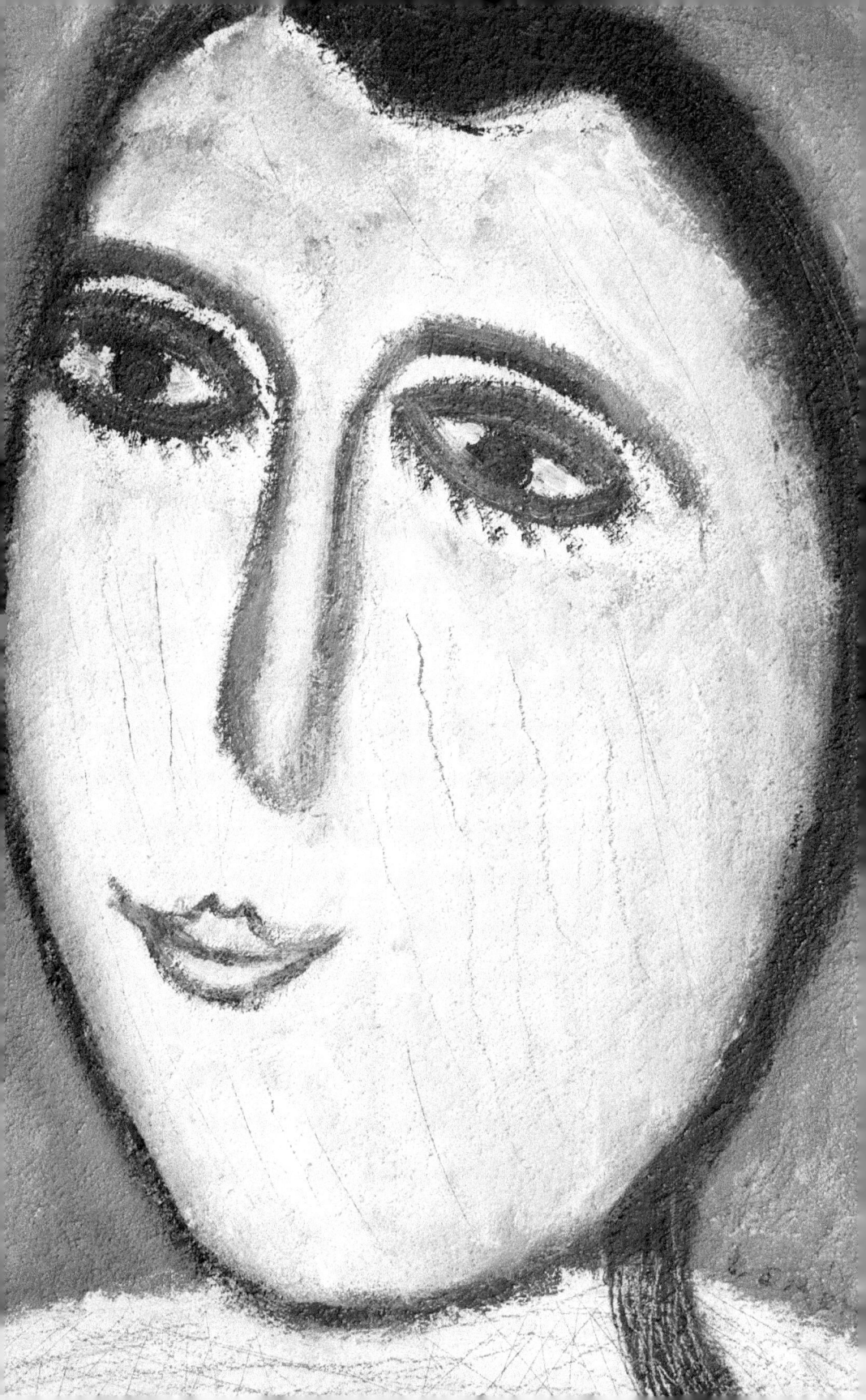

old man DEATH

more friend than enemy

more help than foe

more alive with a new life

than dead with the old

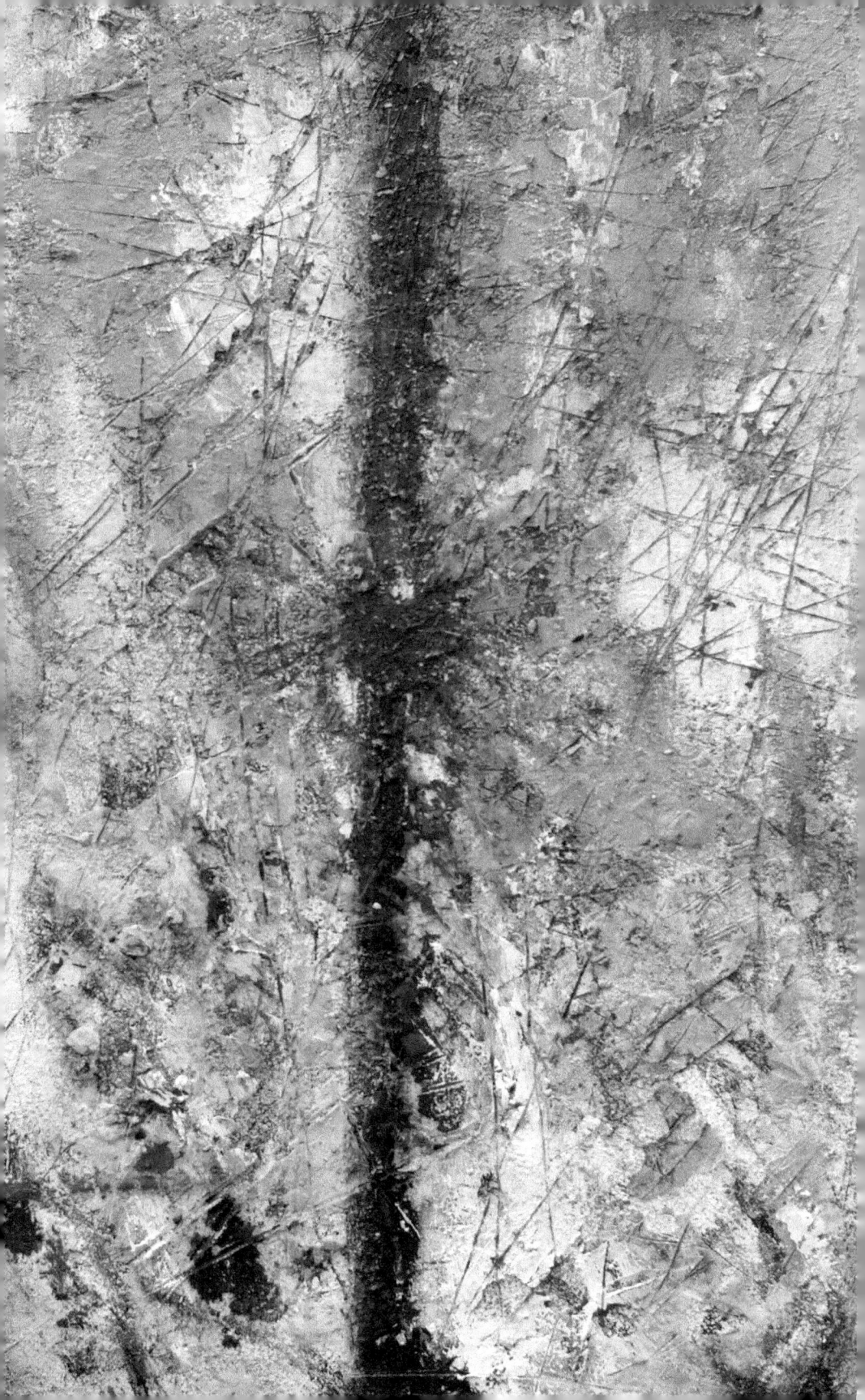

Pain First

He will learn pain first, then relief

He will learn what it is to be a man
And stand up on his own two feet

Life will teach him lessons and emotions
will follow, adults will teach him their ways

Always pain first, like being pulled
from the protection of the womb into the

World with all its problems to solve
And challenges to meet

Pain teaches us lessons, from birth to
the grave

Pleasure teaches too

May we live our lives in pleasure and pain
Peacefully, making the best of
what comes our way

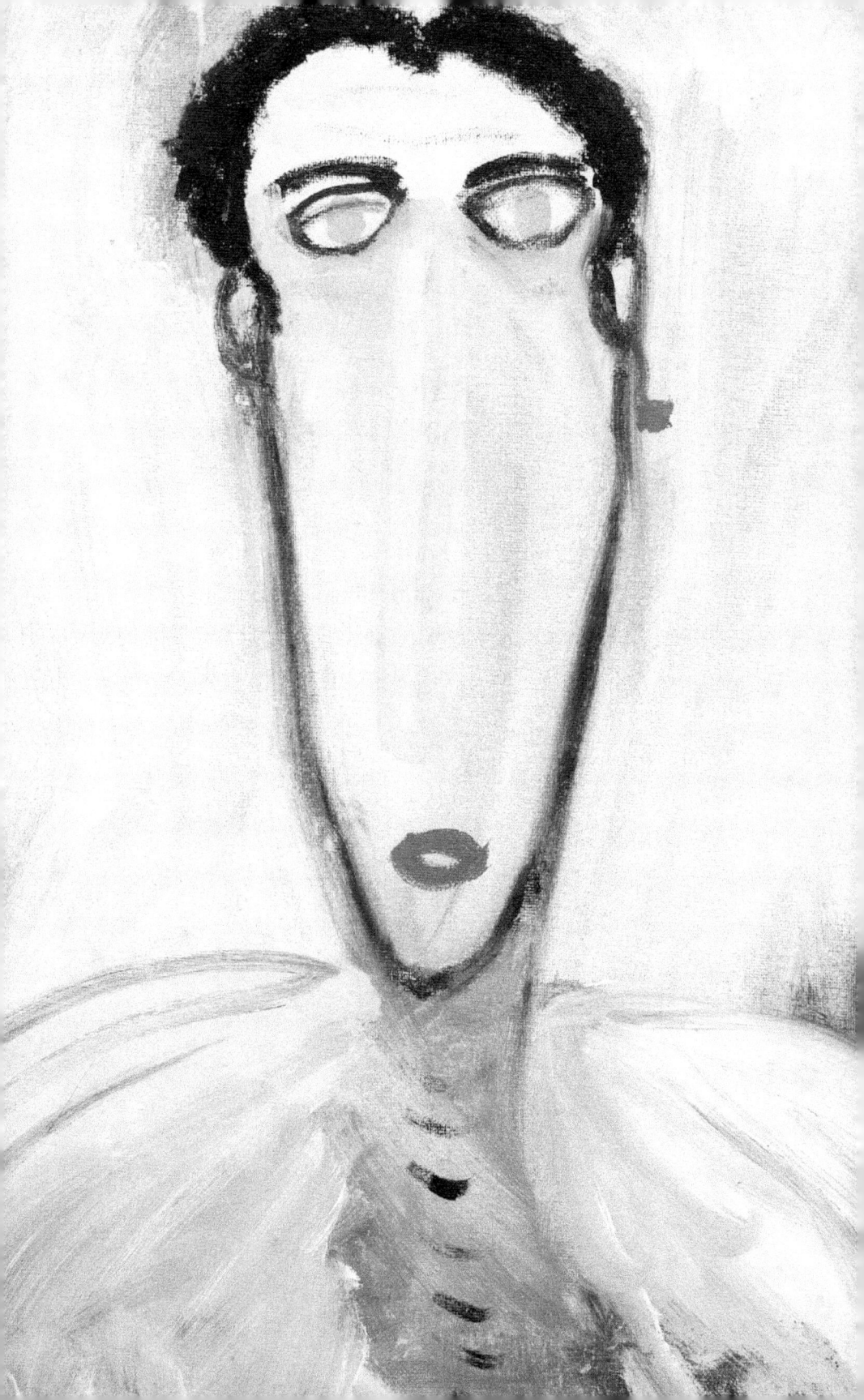

I've got two different
Minds

One, sensitive, contemplative,
Educated, spiritual, sublime, it
Comforts me, makes sense of people and
The world, helps me understand,
My peacemaker

The other mind, crude, uneducated, selfish,
Manipulating me and other people;
Never satisfied with what it sees, always
Critical, tortured and confused,
Forgiveness not its quality, it argues with
Itself incessantly

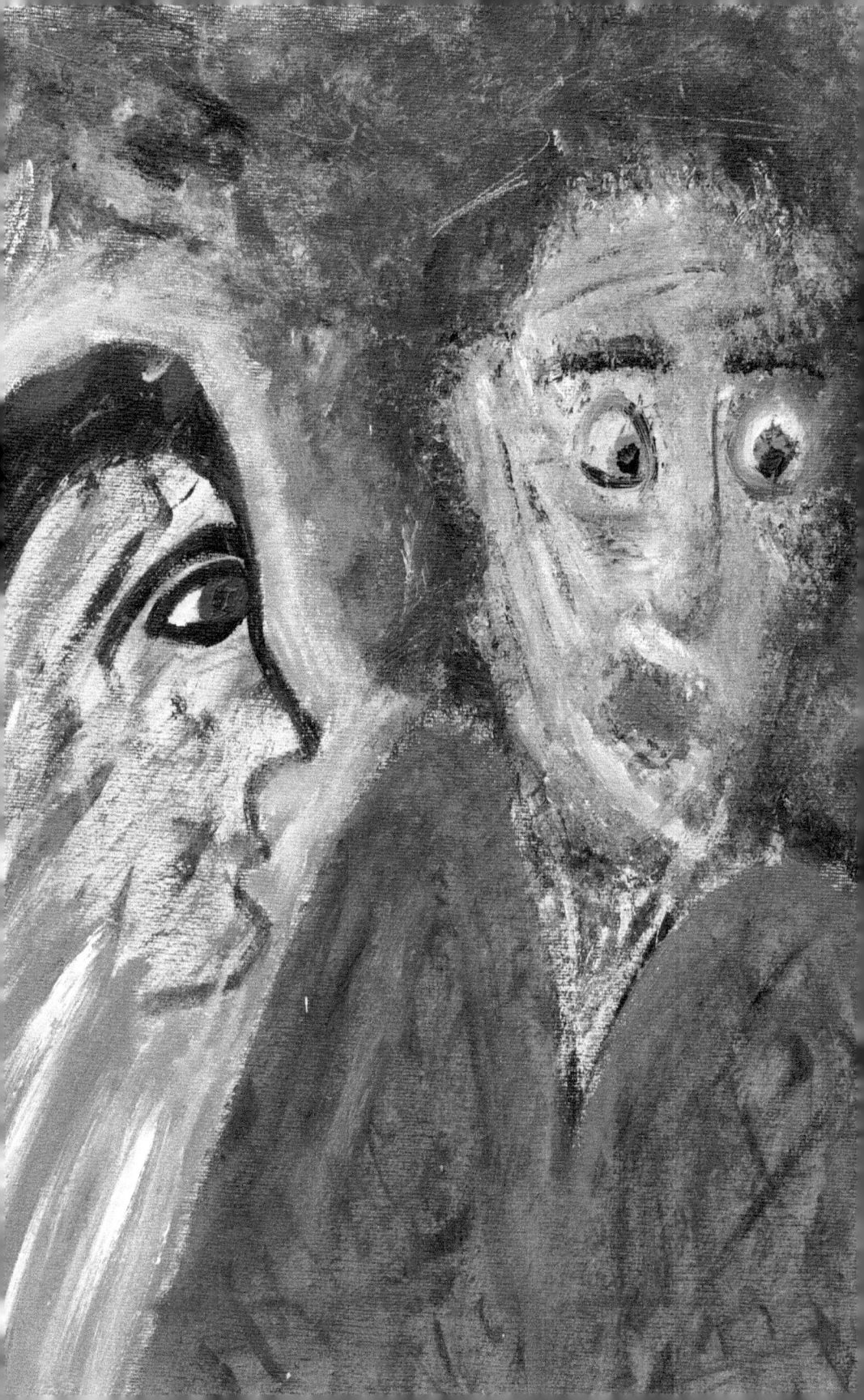

Late at night

I spoke, I cried, I cajoled to the wind as it tossed my
Words to the sea and back to me

Am I good enough? Is all this work painting and writing
Good enough for anyone to care about what I'm trying to give?

To leave behind, or will it all go into some pile of rubble,
Is all this really worth doing?

I feel so lost and inadequate every time I contemplate trying to sell
Anything I create. Please help me.

And the wind held me and rocked me and the ocean mirrored back
The moon and the stars for me to paint and I felt God love me and
urge me

To continue using the gifts so freely given and I am convinced for
Me (and for you) there is no other way to live despite all possible
Outcomes

We must be exactly who we are and do exactly what we feel most
Drawn to do if we are to fulfill our own unique mission here

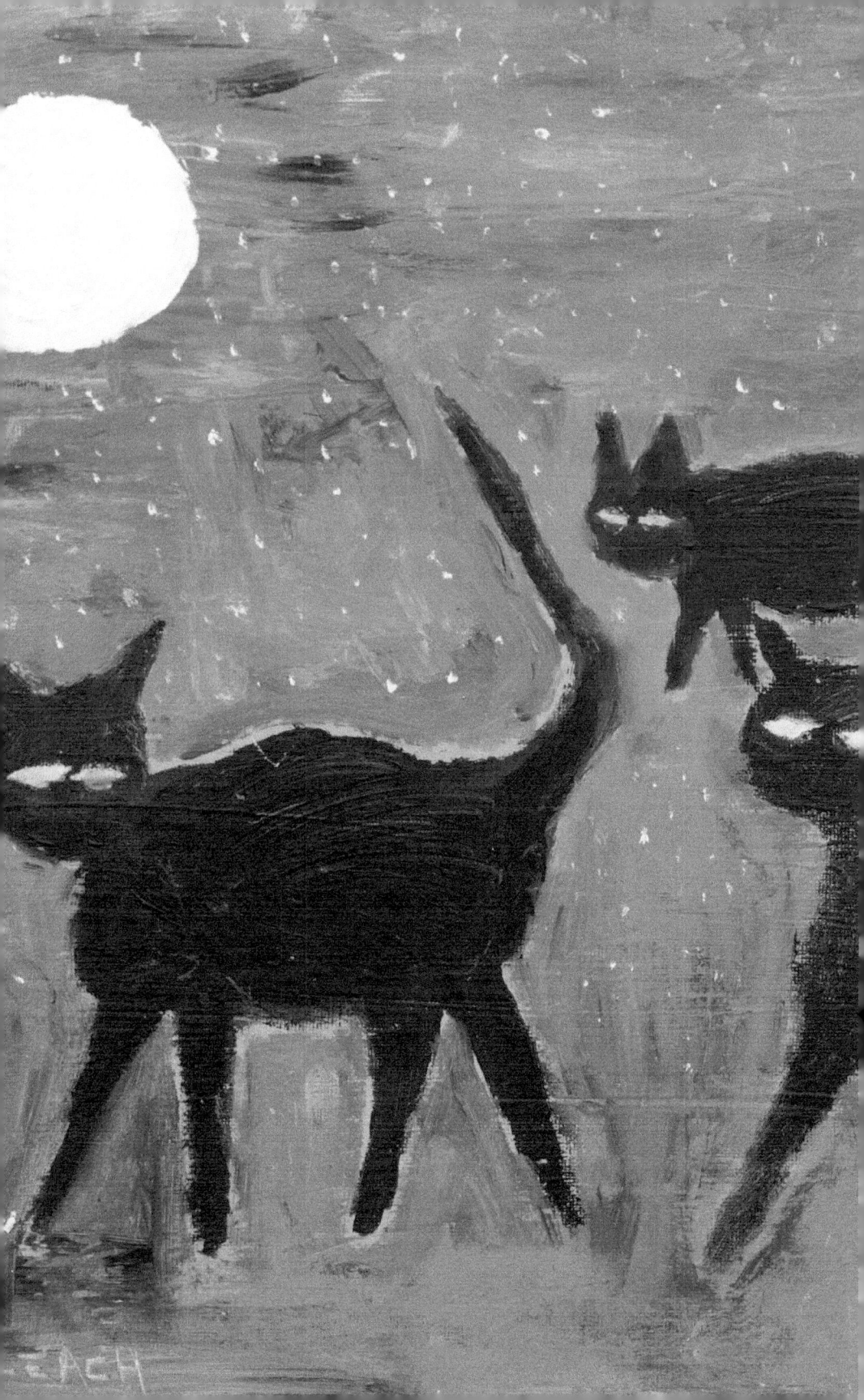

LIFE

You cannot say to your life
More life, less life
Or, more joy, less sorrow
You cannot control life
Life is what life is
Going at its own pace
In its own time, always life
To do with as we will
To share our experiences
And burdens with each other
Until we die
Then you cannot say to your life
More life
Instead, thank You God for
This gift of life…

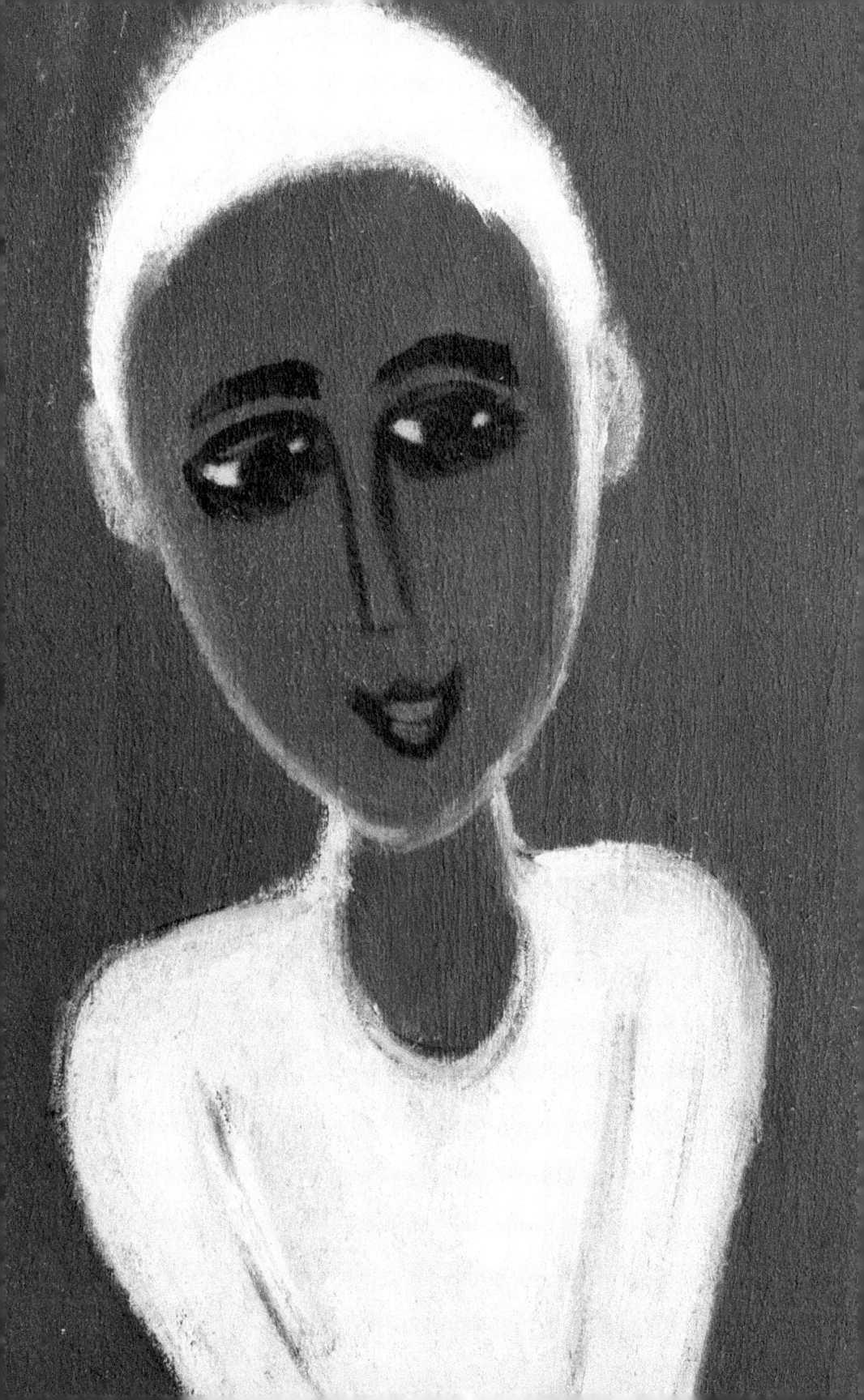

I BELIEVE

We are all parts of the whole

Little self-contained grains of the divine

Functioning in our own vessels of life

Carrying within our beings that which many

Call Great Spirit

Separate while in this life, learning what we are here to know

As whatever forms of life we are

Human, plant, microscopic, tree, lichen

And the other forms, star, rock, water, light, mineral, air

We exist as though we are separate yet surely part of the whole

big thing, I ask the divine to help me give to other life

And to you meaningful acts of kindness

Love and service learning what I am here

To learn so I can contribute what is my

Part to give back

What I lack I receive from others

Impressed by their warm glow and talents

I do not have

What gifts I've been so freely given I

Gratefully give back to You in Your many

Varied forms…

YARROW

"Where does it hurt?"

"Excuse me?"

"Well, you say it hurts so bad. Where does it hurt?"

"All over, damn you for asking such a silly question, it hurts all over."
That's what it is like sometimes, this being alive. It hurts so bad all over,
inside, where I feel, it just fucking hurts. And some days there is no relief,
or so it seems.

And I remember "this too shall pass," things will change, and I'll stop
hurting.

Often it's not the physical pain, though that happens, of course. But the
stuff, the emotional pain, that is what kicks my butt most often. And all this
is part of being human, part of me.

I've even asked several doctors about pills that would help, "you are not
clinically depressed."

I wonder if plants feel this malaise, this disease, is it only a human thing?
Does yarrow suffer too as it makes its little white flowers and goes to seed,
or is it only me in my disease of wanting to feel no pain?

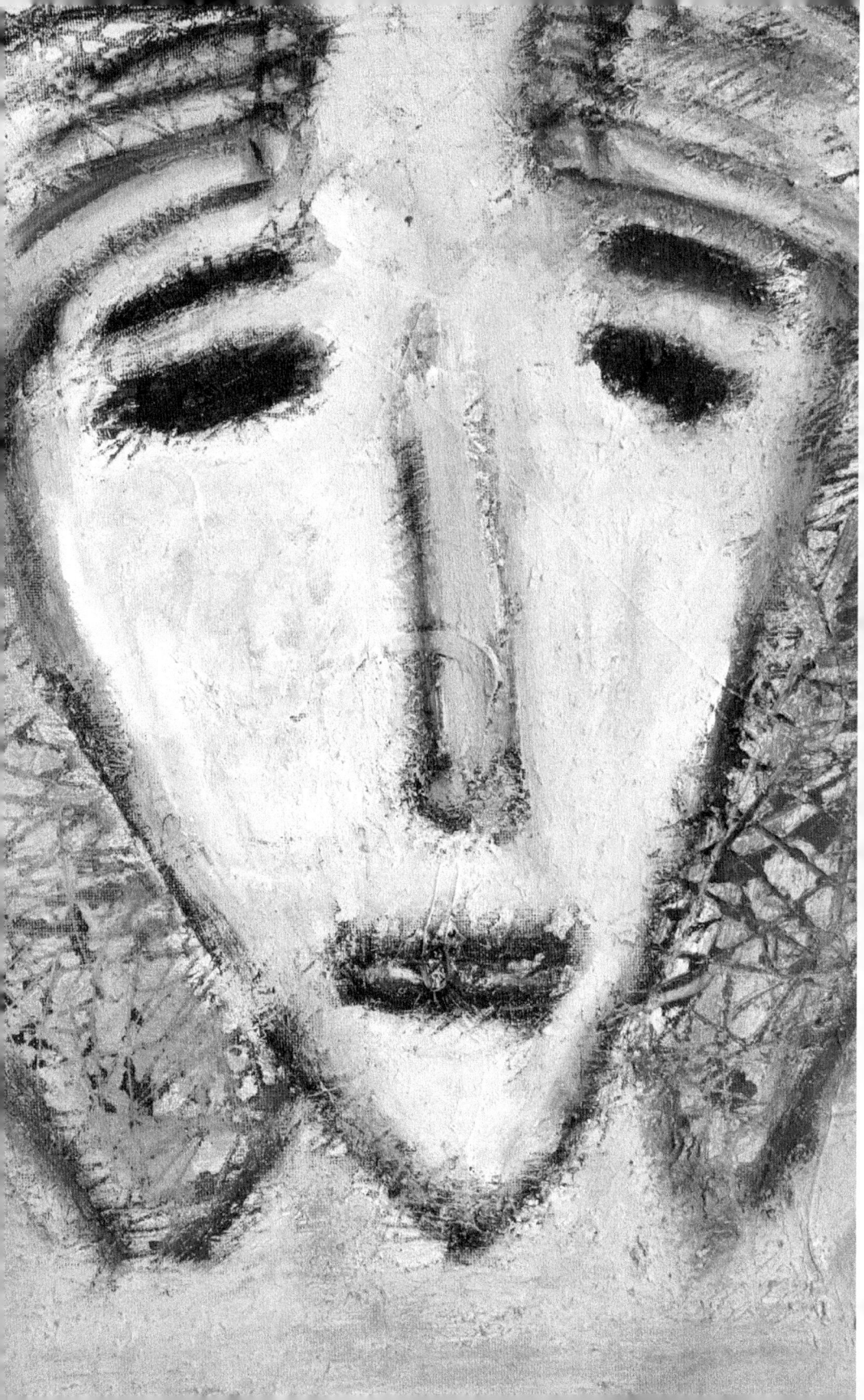

I AM A BROKEN MAN

I crack, fall down

get up

moan and groan

life goes on

doesn't stop

just gets older

I do the best I can

Relax

it's no big deal

one foot out in front

the other follows

this broken vessel

serves me well

it heals

goes on another

I crack, fall down

get up

a broken man

this body serves me well

it just gets older

Wiser now, it carries on

the best it can

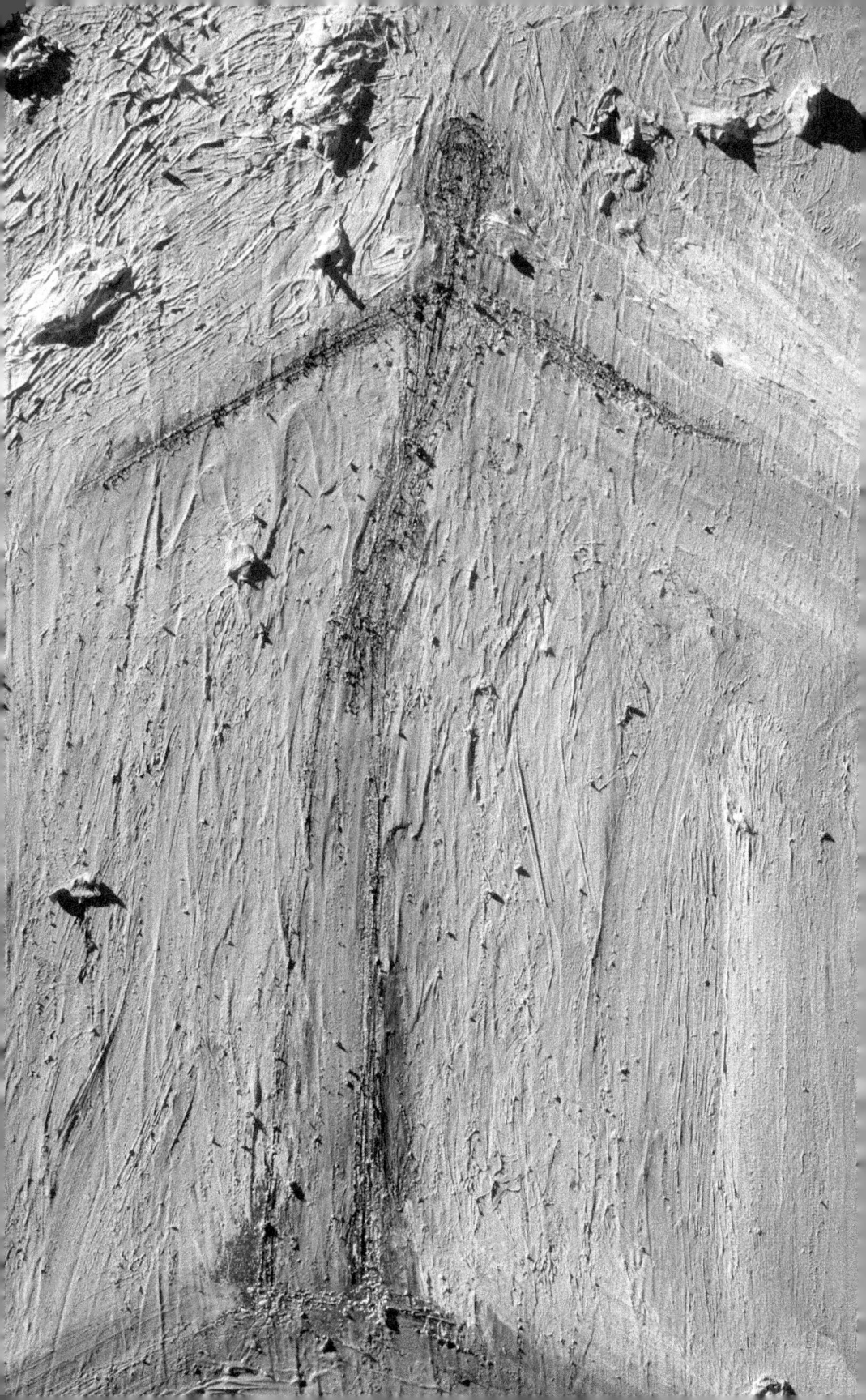

my prayer (to those contemplating suicide)

life is what it is
a great mystery
delicious
compelling
challenging
intimidating
so easily confused
with other things
with other people
this is my prayer for you
that you enjoy your life
seek help you need
not try to extinguish
or drink or drug or throw
your gift away
as I once did
so grateful
I live now
though once I wanted

to end

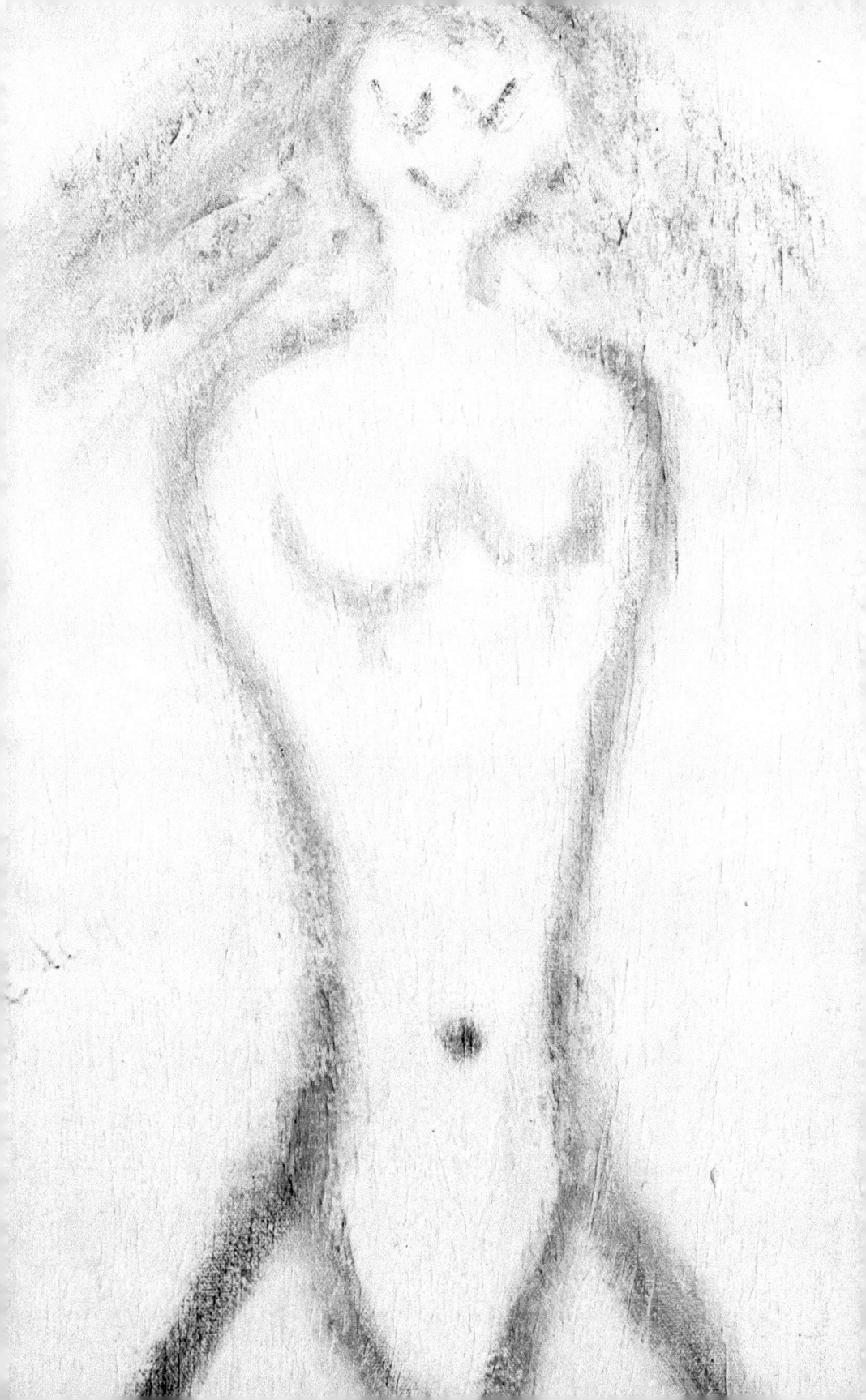

Gratitude

Being alive
Healthy, sober
A free man
Creating
Feeling God's presence
Is enough
To last
A lifetime

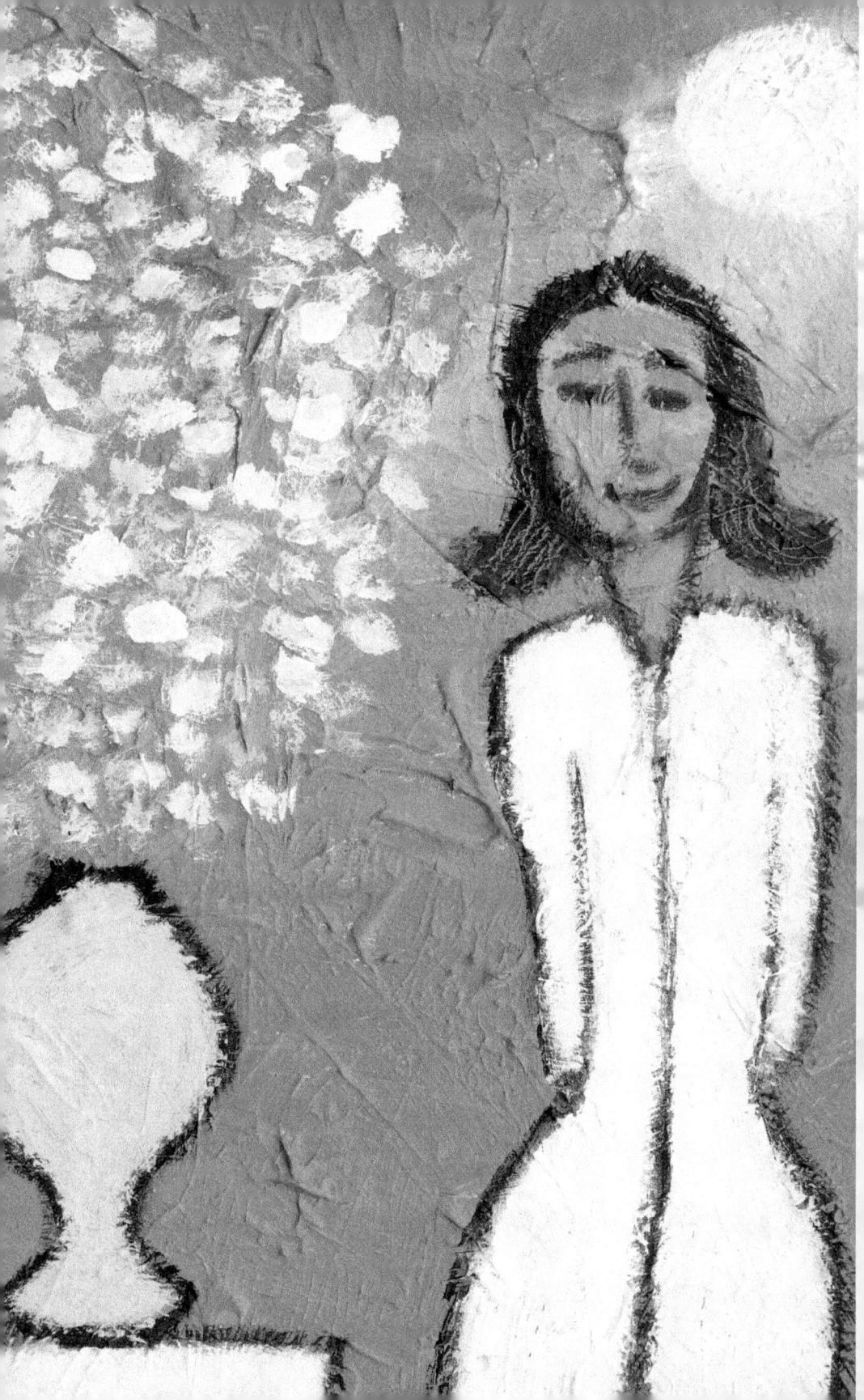

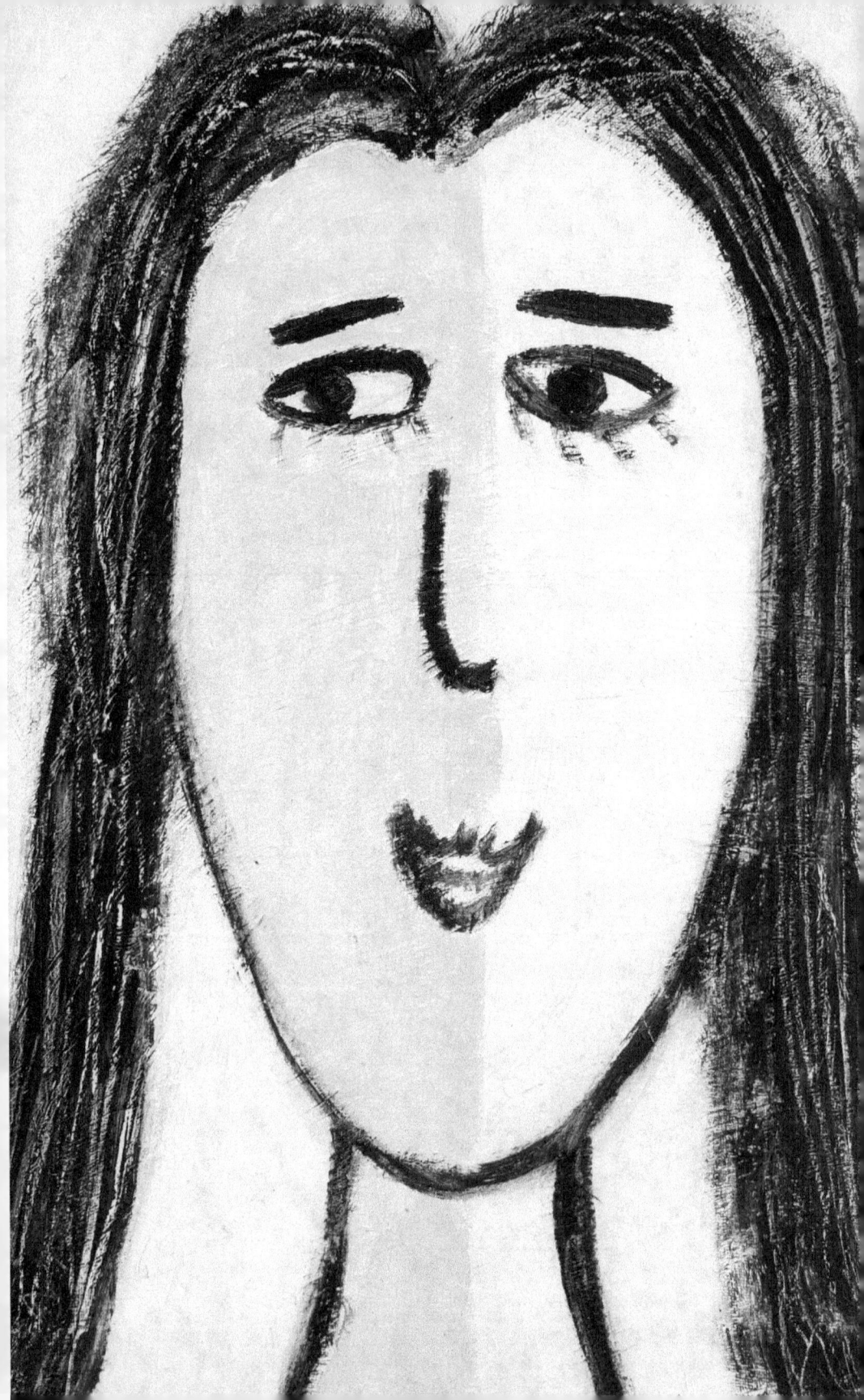

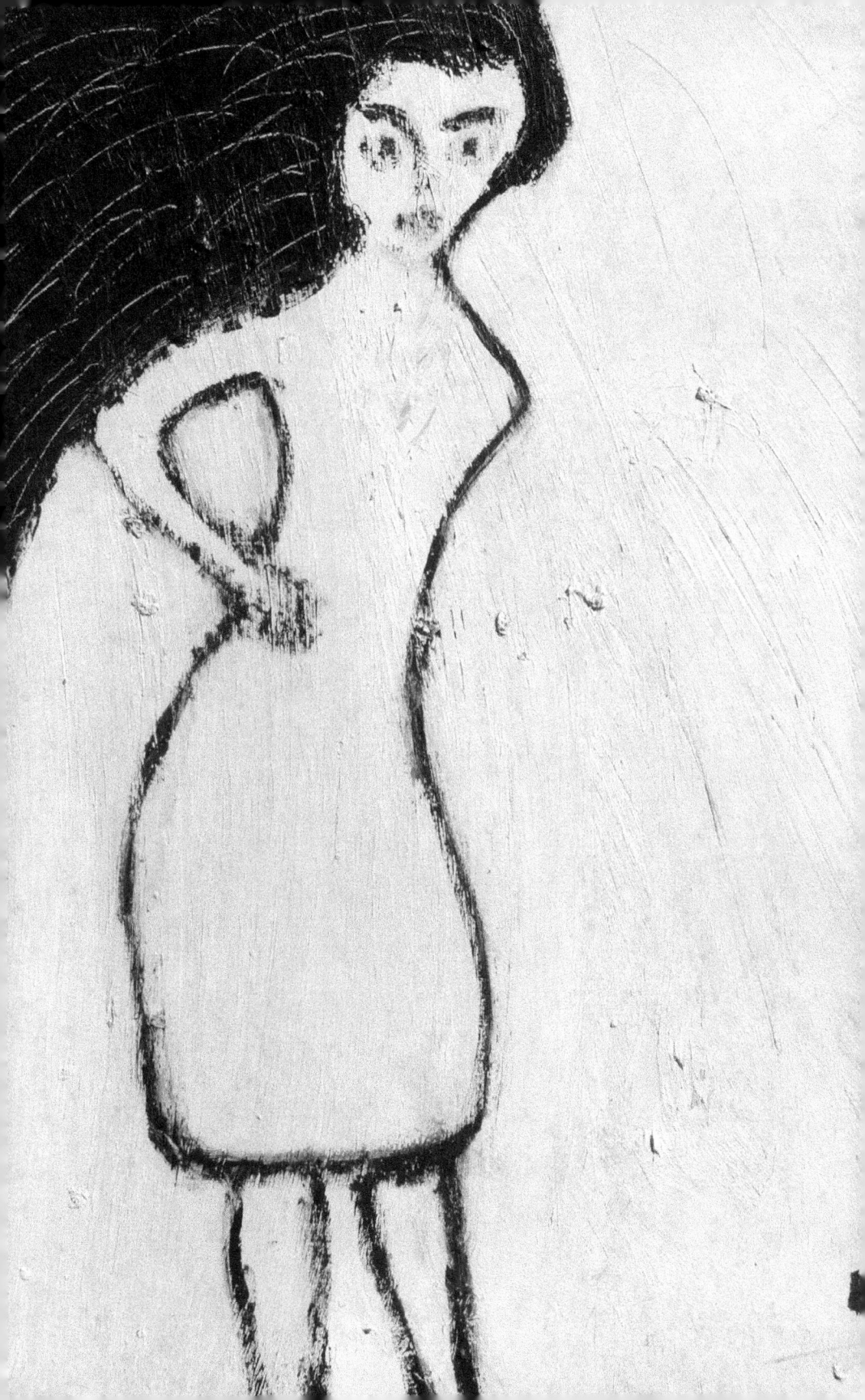

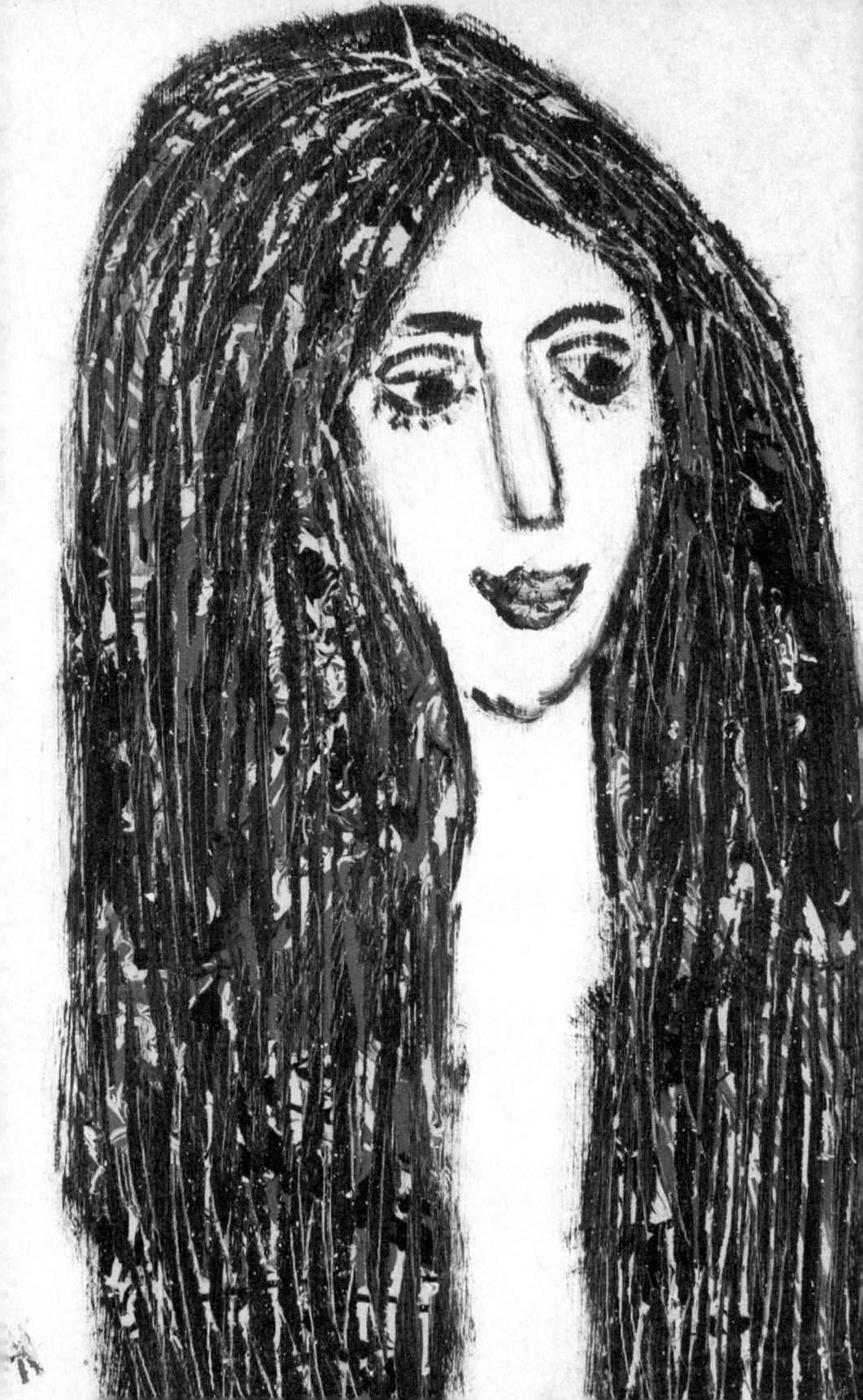

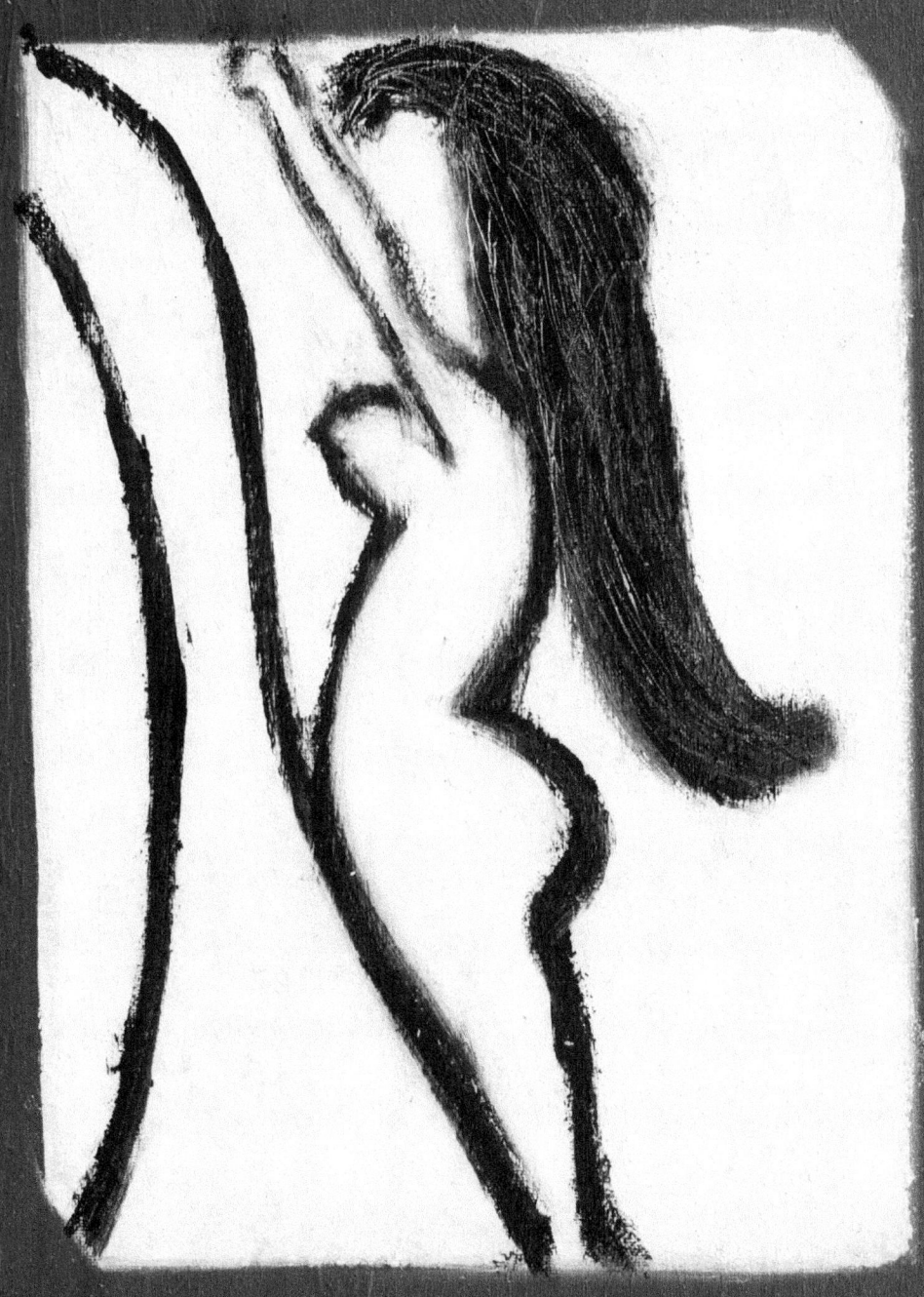

LEACH

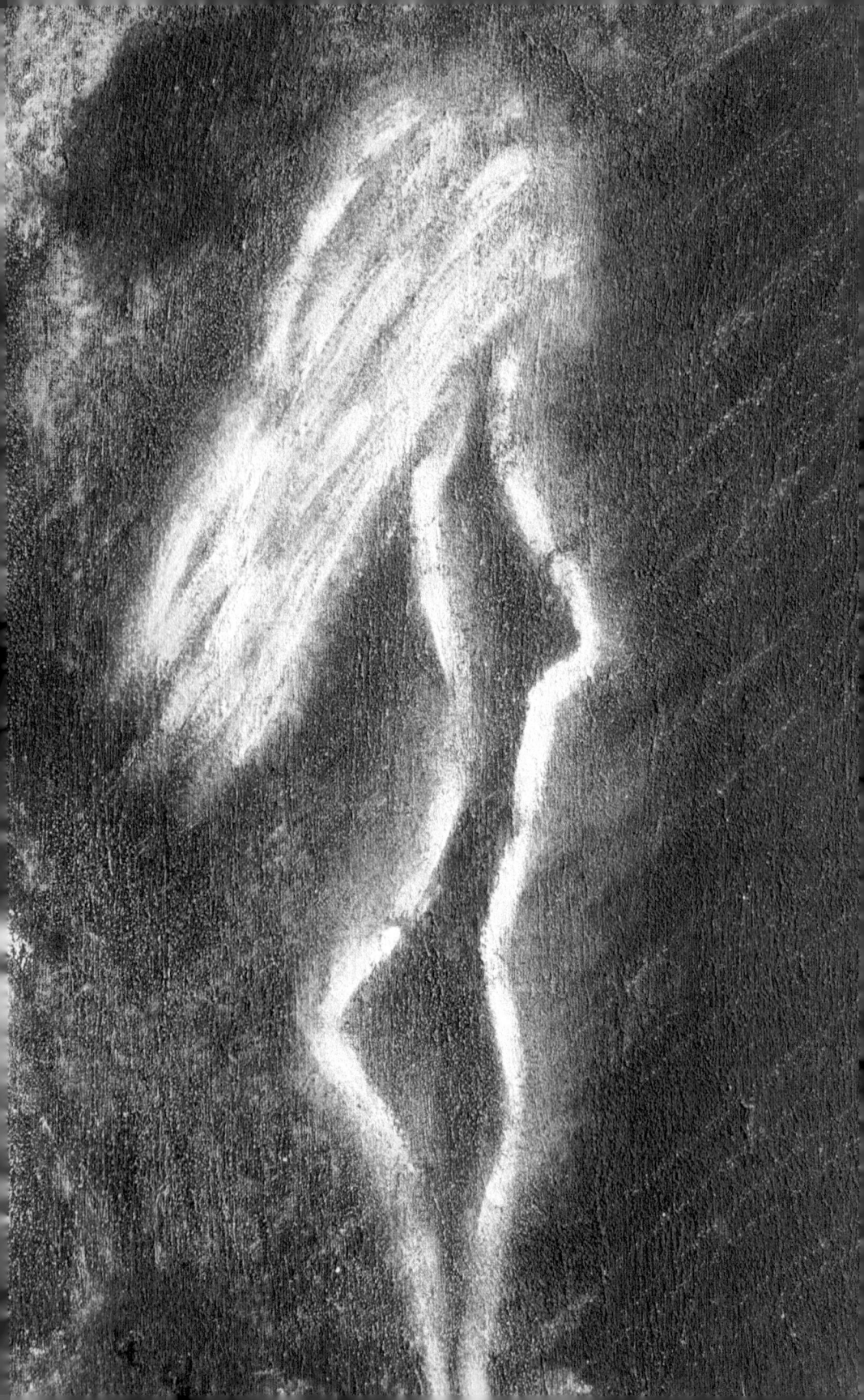

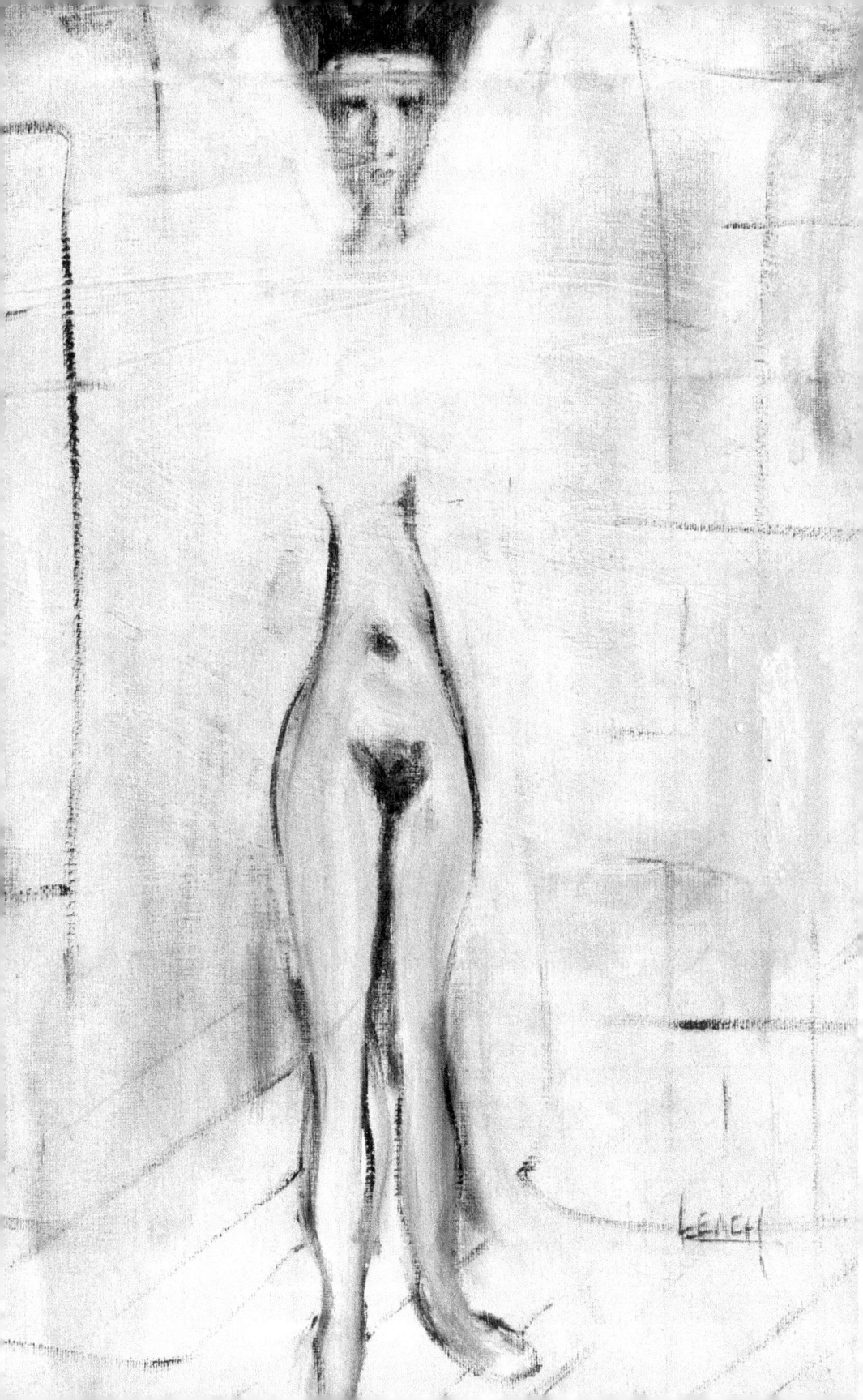

Index of Paintings

Index of Paintings *(continued)*

Index of Paintings *(continued)*

Index of Paintings *(continued)*

Index of Paintings *(continued)*

Index of Paintings *(continued)*

the

END

for now

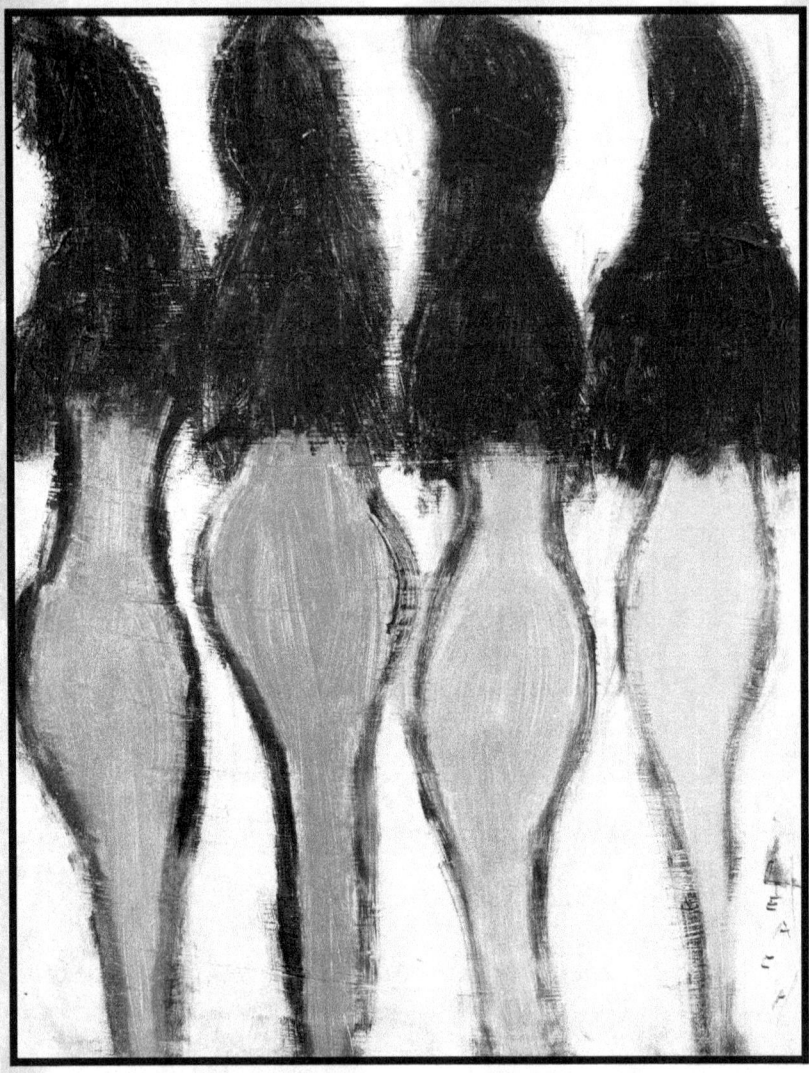

Color Test Pattern, 2007
16" x 20"
acrylic / canvas

visit me at   patleachartist.com

www.ingramcontent.com/pod-product-compliance
Lightning Source LLC
Chambersburg PA
CBHW051326170526
45166CB00002B/700